TAROT READING FOR DUMMIES

Beginner's Guide to Understanding Tarot Cards and Their Meanings, Psychic Tarot Reading, Simple Tarot Spreads, History, Symbolism and Divination

Shelly O'Bryan

Copyright 2019 by Shelly O'Bryan - All rights reserved.

No part of this book may be reproduced or transmitted in any form or by any means, electronic or mechanical, including photocopying, recording or by any information storage and retrieval system without written permission of the publisher, except for the inclusion of brief quotations in a review.

This content is provided with the sole purpose of providing relevant information on a specific topic for which every reasonable effort has been made to ensure that it is both accurate and reasonable. Nevertheless, by purchasing this content you consent to the fact that the author, as well as the publisher, are in no way experts on the topics contained herein, regardless of any claims as such that may be made within. As such, any suggestions or recommendations that are made within are done so purely for entertainment value. It is recommended that you always consult a professional prior to undertaking any of the advice or techniques discussed within.

This is a legally binding declaration that is considered both valid and fair by both the
Committee of Publishers Association and the American Bar Association and should be considered as legally binding within the United States.

The reproduction, transmission, and duplication of any of the content found herein, including any specific or extended information will be done as an illegal act regardless of the end form the information ultimately takes. This includes copied versions of the work both physical, digital and audio unless express consent of the Publisher is provided beforehand. Any additional rights reserved.

Furthermore, the information that can be found within the pages described forthwith shall be considered both accurate and truthful when it comes to the recounting of facts.
As such, any use, correct or incorrect, of the provided information will render the Publisher free of responsibility as to the actions taken outside of their direct purview. Regardless, there are zero scenarios where the original author or the Publisher can be deemed

liable in any fashion for any damages or hardships that may result from any of the information discussed herein.

Additionally, the information in the following pages is intended only for informational purposes and should thus be thought of as universal. As befitting its nature, it is presented without assurance regarding its prolonged validity or interim quality. Trademarks that are mentioned are done without written consent and can in no way be considered an endorsement from the trademark holder.

TABLE OF CONTENTS

Introduction 1
Chapter 1 *Defining Tarot* 2
Chapter 2 *What's The Point?* 4
Chapter 3 *Fact Or Fiction* 6
Chapter 4 *Getting Started* 8
Chapter 5 *All About The Cards* 10
Chapter 6 *Cards Meanings* 25
Chapter 7 *The Lay Of The Land* 85
Chapter 8 *What Am I Doing?* 93
Chapter 9 *Practice Makes Perfect* 95
Chapter 10 *Incorporating The Cards In Your Life* 97
Conclusion 99

INTRODUCTION

Dear Reader,

Firstly, I would like to personally thank you for purchasing my book. Second, as the name implies, this book is to be used as a beginner's guide to the understanding of Tarot cards and their many uses. That being said, this book can and will help anyone, regardless of skill level, even that of total mastery.

This book will define and explain Tarot, its usage in divination, and the odd history behind it. It will debunk some common misconceptions about Tarot as well as assist you in getting started. Further into the book, you will learn, in great detail, what each card looks like in the original Rider-Waite deck along with the meanings of each card when drawn either upright or reversed. You will also be given an in depth explanation of the symbolism behind the illustrations of each card in this deck.

Finally, you will be given some example Tarot spreads and tips to mastering the art of divination through Tarot reading.

CHAPTER 1
Defining Tarot

According to Merriam Webster, Tarot is simply defined as any of a set of usually 78 playing cards including 22 pictorial cards used for fortune-telling. However, we know Tarot to be much more personal than that.

Tarot is, in short, a divination tool used to help guide us on the right or most beneficial path in life. It is used when you are forced to make a difficult decision, or just when you do not know which way to turn, which path to take.

The truth is, however, Tarot didn't start as a divination tool. It started as early as 1375 as a normal deck of playing cards. They were used to play a game similar to bridge called "triumph". Unlike bridge, though, this game used 78 cards: 4 suits labeled Ace-10, Page, Knight, Queen, and King, & 22 cards that didn't belong to one of the four suits.

In current usage, each suit represents an element. Swords are air, Wands are fire, Cups are water, and Pentacles are earth. They are used for more minor or hidden answers, while the 22 cards of the major arcana are typically used for major decisions and important information.

One theory on the origin of the divination usage of Tarot was likely around 1781, several hundred years later. The deck was found in Europe by occult followers. They drew symbolic meaning from the cards and felt that the Divine had placed those meanings on the cards for guidance.

Another theory assumes that Tarot cards escaped from the fires that burned the libraries of Egypt, and resurfaced in the year 1781 when a French Freemason wrote about their hidden meanings. He thought that they were hieroglyphs spelling out the key to life.

The most widely known Tarot deck is the Rider-Waite deck. It is not only the most widely sold but also one of the original designs based on the original deck. It was first created in 1909 and is the deck we will be describing in chapter 5.

There are suggested meanings that we will go over in chapter 6, but ultimately, it is a connection between you and the Divine or your inner wisdom.

CHAPTER 2
What's The Point?

Though many people use Tarot readings, several do not know everything a reading can do to help. Most beginners have several false impressions, outlined in Chapter 3, but let's start by explaining the most basic ways Tarot readings can help you in your day to day life.

Guidance

The most notable and well recognized of the uses of a deck, Tarot readings, in their most basic form, are to provide guidance. You go into a Tarot reading with a question in mind. These questions can be anything under the sun with no regard to the magnitude of the said question. It can be as specific as "how can I find a new job," or as broad as "what does my life hold in store", as important as "should I break up with my significant other," or as mundane as "should I carpool today". This is the purpose of everyone who uses Tarot knows, beginners to masters. However, it is not the only purpose.

Decision-Making

Another common use of the deck is simple decision-making. Some people have trouble figuring out what they want to do with their day and use the cards to aid in this process. Your question comprises of two or more options, and while the answer usually is not direct, the cards will help lead you to a decision. These decisions can be as life-changing as "should I move to Japan or England" or as simple as "should I get a sandwich or salad for lunch". This could fall under the category of guidance, and many people bunch the two together because of their similarities. However, I feel the guidance category is more open-ended. There aren't set options like with questions in this category.

Comfort

One use that not many people know or talk about is using the deck to bring comfort. If you are worried about a decision you have to make but know your answer already, you can ask a question as simple as "is this the right choice?" and interpret your card(s) for that question. It can also bring comfort for the future. A question as simple as "on my current path, what does the future hold" can assure you that everything will be fine, or alternatively, make you aware of a problem that needs to be solved for your current situation to end.

CHAPTER 3
Fact Or Fiction

Myth 1: Tarot is evil

Many people try to tie Tarot and the occult to the devil based on their portrayal in popular media. This is one of the first myths we must debunk as it holds no truth whatsoever. Uninformed individuals like to say that Tarot will make people's lives miserable. That could not be further from the truth. Tarot is used almost exclusively to *help people* make decisions or gain knowledge that they may otherwise be too overwhelmed or even scared to pursue. Even "spooky" cards like Death or the Hanged Man are nothing to fear. We'll cover the meanings of these cards, along with the rest, in chapter 6.

Myth 2: The answers Tarot gives will be obvious

This is not entirely false, as sometimes the answer will seem to jump at you from the cards laying before you. More often though, you will have to do some form of search within yourself in order to see the answers the cards are trying to give. This is discouraging to some, but I promise with work and practice, you will develop a knack for reading what the cards have to offer.

Myth 3: Things will change overnight

As with anything in life, you must work for change. The cards simply offer possibilities for how to attain a goal and suggestions for what you need to do. They are guidance. You still must take control of your own path in life.

Myth 4: There's a certain way to read Tarot

Given that Tarot reading is such a personal skill, no one can dictate the right or wrong way to read the cards. As stated before, the purpose of Tarot is to provide guidance. As such, the things that pop out to you in your readings may not be the same that pop out for everyone and may even change from one reading to the next.

Do not be discouraged if your reading ends up not being accurate or the one you hoped for. The cards will be interpreted by each person in a different way. Keep your head up and keep practicing. The only "wrong" way to read Tarot is to not read it at all.

Myth 5: In order to read Tarot, you must be deeply involved in the occult

I do not think I need to explain why this is incorrect. It is just a method of guidance. Yes, it has some ties to the occult, but there's no reason you must be deeply involved or even relate to any occult. For many people, Tarot reading is what draws them closer to the occult or their path with the Divine. However, the occult is just one part of how people use Tarot cards. For many, it can be very spiritual and provide guidance with no ties to any occult.

CHAPTER 4
Getting Started

Choosing a deck

Many people feel you need to get the original Rider-Waite deck, but this is not the case. Get the deck to which you feel drawn. It is generally best to find these in a store, but some people can feel immediately drawn to a deck sold online. There are also Tarot card apps, but many people believe that the Divine won't interact as personally through a mobile app. However, do not go broke trying to get the "perfect deck". If you do not have any extra spending money, go for an app to get your feet wet in readings and buy your deck when you can. Also, some people are driven to get an application because they feel a pull to it. If this is you, do not worry about what other people say about applications. There's no right or wrong way to do Tarot. This includes the deck you choose to use.

Choosing a spread

First and foremost, you should base the spread you use on your need. Chapter 7 has some example spreads, but many can be found with a quick search online. The ones covered in that chapter are simply some of the most common. If you need a spread for romance, choose a spread you feel will cover your question thoroughly. The same can be said for any topic imaginable. Most spreads have suggested usage but can easily be adapted to any question you may have. Use the spreads you feel pulled to in order to answer your question.

Secondly, choose a spread based on the time and space you have available. If you are on the go or do not have time to do a full spread, use the one card method. If you have a large amount of time and space or a more complex question, use a larger spread to make sure you cover all your bases.

Setting up your space

I will reiterate this as much as needed, but there is no wrong way to read Tarot. If you want to set up an altar devoted to your readings, do so. If you can only do the reading on the dining room table, that is perfectly fine. Many people like to include an idol to the Divine and crystals such as clear quartz or amethyst to focus the energy of the Divine to thoroughly answer their question. Others use candles or crystals directly related to their question. Others keep a deck in their bag and draw cards as needed throughout the day. I really can't state enough that the only "wrong" way to do readings is to not do them at all.

CHAPTER 5
All About The Cards

Tarot cards are separated into two groups: Major Arcana and Minor Arcana. Please note that the descriptions of these cards are based on a standard deck, though there are specialized decks as well, each with their own designs.

Major Arcana

The major arcana are the cards people most often think of when picturing a Tarot deck. There are 22 cards that count as "Major Arcana". The name of each is prefaced by a number, generally written in Roman numerals.

0 The Fool
Sometimes labeled as "The Jester", this card has a man in a fancy coat and cap holding a pack, thrown over his shoulder, and a white rose. He is standing on a crumbling cliff but seems blissfully unaware of the impending danger he is in. He is looking up, which could be symbolic of looking for new opportunities or being generally optimistic, even when you probably shouldn't. By his feet is a white dog standing on his hind legs in an almost playful stance or, perhaps, to get the attention of the fool to warn him of the danger he is in.

This card is sometimes written without a number at all, lending to the ideas of limitless, though not all practical, possibilities recognized by the fool.

I The Magician
On this card, a man stands behind a table holding what appears to be a white candle over his head. The man is draped in red cloth. On the table in front of him, there is a pentacle, a wand, a sword, and a cup. These four items are the suits of the minor arcana. The man also has an infinity symbol above his head.

This card's design, along with the numeral I, points to the idea that the magician was the first of many things and, perhaps, even chose the symbolism of the minor arcana. This ideology sort of puts the Magician parallel with the Divine.

II The High Priestess
This card features a woman in a fancy light blue dress sitting between two pillars labeled "B" in black and "J" in white. She has a crown reminiscent in shape to the Triple Moon Symbol, representing the Goddess of the moon. She also has a crescent moon at her feet.

This card is all about dichotomies. The "B" on the black pillar is symbolic of the number 2, as it is the second letter in the alphabet. The "J" on the white pillar is symbolic of the number 1. Yes, "J" is the 10th letter of the alphabet, but in numerology, 10 is reduced to 1. The 1 and 2, along with the black and white pillars are meant to represent the God and Goddess of the Divine.

III The Empress
On this card, a woman adorned with a pomegranate-print dress sits atop what seems to be a rocky thrown, covered in red cushions and tapestry. On top of her head is a crown of stars and by her side is a heart-shaped shield emblazoned with the symbol of Venus, more commonly known as a symbol of femininity. Her stance shows power as she embraces all things feminine and beautiful.

IV The Emperor
The Emperor is a white-haired man with a long beard. He is sitting in a rocky thrown embellished with ram skull statuettes. His red drapery allows only his arms and armored legs to stick out. He has a golden crown set with many jewels and is holding a golden scepter in his right hand (on the left of the card). His left hand (on the right of the card) is holding a golden orb.

Many speculate that this is a wiser version of the Magician. If it is, he has aged into a leader who seems to have been hardened by battle. He has an air of command and masculinity about him. This represents the dichotomy of man and woman when compared to the Empress.

V The Hierophant

This card features a man with an ornate, golden crown and red robes holding a scepter in his thrown while two balding men bow before him. On either side of the Hierophant is a stone pillar. Many people believe the crown's 5 points to represent the 5 senses and its 3 tiers to represent the conscious, subconscious, and superconscious state of mind.

VI The Lovers

Adam and Eve are the focus of the bottom half of the card. There's the Tree of Knowledge behind Eve, complete with the Devil in serpent form winding around the trunk. Both Adam and Eve are nude, leading one to think the serpent has not yet succeeded in coaxing the woman. The two humans are looking up to a brightly colored angel, bathing in sunlight, located in the top half of the card.

VII The Chariot

The Charioteer is very androgynous in appearance, with an armored chest plate blocking any form of cleavage that may be used to determine gender. The person is wearing a crown with an 8-pointed sun, reminiscent of a compass's directions, and a cloak which features a crescent moon on each shoulder. They are holding a short spear, clearly ready to ride into battle. In front of the Chariot, perhaps pulling it, are two sphinxes, one black and one white. The dichotomy of colors represents that the Charioteer has both masculine and feminine features. Behind them is the city they were sworn to protect.

VIII Strength

This card shows a feminine individual forcing or coaxing the jaws of a lion closed. The person has an infinity symbol above their head as a symbol of eternity or immortality. Their white dress is covered in flowers and a crown of the same flowers is placed upon their head. Though one hand is on the upper and lower jaw of the lion involved, they seem calm and not forceful. This is to show that strength not only comes in the form of raw power but also control and willpower.

IX The Hermit
The Hermit is a wise and greyed old man, adorned in grey robes, holding a staff and lantern. Nothing is visible in the background besides from a small, lonely tree. The ground beneath him is pure white, adding to the feeling of solitude.

X Wheel of Fortune
In the center of the card is a wheel, with the letters ROMA spanning the length of the circumference. The word is Roman for "the wheel". Among the clouds surrounding the wheel are several creatures. These include a red, dog-faced devil creature, a serpent, a sphinx grasping a sword, a swan, an angel, a winged bull, and a winged lion. The last four of the list are each reading a book.

XI Justice
The woman on this card wears red robes and a three-pronged crown. In her left hand, she holds a scale, a common symbol of justice and equality. In her right, she wields a sword, ready to punish wrongdoers. She sits in a stone throne, ready for the next of the accused to plead their case at her feet.

XII The Hanged Man
The man, presumably one of holy nature, given the halo around his head, wears a blue shirt and red pants with a belt tied around the waist. He is hanging by one foot tied to a log with his hands tied behind his back. The imagery parallels that of the Christian Jesus but ends in a less gruesome sight.

XIII Death
Death rides on a white stallion, his skull face poking out from a full suit of armor. He carries a black flag with a white, 5-petaled flower and the numeral XIII. Under the feet of the horse, a well-dressed body lies face down. In front, a child sits on his knees as a man in golden garb tries to plead with death to spare the child. Another body sits against a rock directly behind the child.

XIV Temperance
We yet again see the angel from card VI The Lovers. This time, they float above a small body of water surrounded by brush. They are pouring water from one cup to another, bringing the dichotomy from card VI to a sense of oneness.

XV The Devil
The immediate eye-catcher of this card is the devil, who is given the head and two legs of a ram, the feet and wings of a bat, and the torso of a man. In his left hand is a torch, representing hellfire. Between his horns is an inverted pentacle and at his perched feet are Adam and Eve, chained to his pedestal. They both have tails and horns, alluding to the idea that they let their beastly desires lead them to captivity. The background is completely black.

XVI The Tower
Central to this card is the tower, whose large golden crown has been shot off by an arrow of lightning. The lightning sets the tower itself on fire. Two people can be seen leaping from the tower, seeing falling to their possible demise as more opportune than being caught in the lighting and fire.

This card in its entirety seems to represent royalty being struck down by the Divine and the people of said royalty abandoning the monarch in a sense of self-protection.

XVII The Star
A nude woman stands below a large, golden 8-point star surrounded by 7 smaller white ones. She is filling the lakes and rivers with water from her copper pots. In the distance, a bird sits atop a single tree on a hill.

XVIII The Moon
The moon, personified with a woman's face, sits between two towers. Though in the distance, it is a looming presence on the card. A coyote and dog are howling at her as a lobster climbs from the water at the base of the card.

XIX The Sun
The sun, personified with a man's face, shines down over sunflowers and a playful boy. The boy is nude, riding a white horse, and holding a red tapestry.

XX Judgement
In this card, an angel blows the horn of Revelations as corpses, adult and child alike, climb out of their coffins. The most saturated

color is found in the angel above, giving the idea that things up there are far better than things down here.

XXI The World
The last of the major arcana, The World shows a nude woman holding a scepter in each hand. A grey cloth wraps loosely around her form. Surrounding her is a green wreath, with red ribbons at the top and bottom, mirroring the North and South Pole. There are four clouds on the card, one on each corner. On the clouds, starting with the top left and continuing clockwise, are a man's head, a bird's head, a lion's head, and a bull's head.

Minor Arcana

The Minor Arcana consists of 56 cards separated into four suits, Swords, Wands, Cups, and Pentacles. Each suit has 14 cards. They are Ace/1, 2-10, Page, Knight, Queen, and King. Each card implements their suit into the design and the number of the card if applicable.

The Swords Suit

The Swords Suit is considered interchangeable with the Spade suit in a normal deck of cards.

Ace
This card features a white hand coming from storm clouds over an ocean. The hand is holding a sword with a crown on top. Draped from the crown are two types of greenery.

Two
A blindfolded woman holds two swords across her chest. She sits atop a box with the sea behind her. In the sky is a crescent moon.

Three
Three swords are run through a heart. In the background, rain clouds fill the sky, giving a heavy downpour.

Four

A man lies on a platform in a church setting with his hands across his chest. In the upper left is a stained-glass window depicting a holy man giving to an older woman. Above the man hang three swords with a fourth below him on the platform.

Five
Two men have dropped their swords and are walking to the sea in the background. A third, adorned in a green tunic, red undershirt, red pants, and brown boots has been picking up discarded swords and currently holds three.

Six
A shrouded figure and child are being rowed across a body of water in a boat. The rower is a man standing with a long oar, propelling them forward. At the front of the ship, six swords are standing, hilt skyward.

Seven
A man carrying five swords sneaks away from an encampment, happy with the loot he has stolen. The tents of the encampment can be seen in the background. Two swords have been stuck in the ground.

Eight
A woman in red stands tied up and blindfolded. In the background is the silhouette of a castle. Eight swords have been stabbed into the ground around her.

Nine
A young man is sitting upright in bed after a nightmare. His quilt is adorned with rose patterns and zodiac symbols. Carved into his bed is a battle and above his bed hang nine swords.

Ten
A man lies bloodied on the ground face down, as ten swords protrude from his back. The sky is black to show the death surrounding the man.

Page

A young man stands over rolling hills, wielding a sword. He has an air of confidence, or perhaps arrogance, about him.

Knight
A man rides valiantly into battle atop his white steed. His is in full armor with a red plume and cape.

Queen
A woman adorned in a cloud-printed robe and white dress motions for someone to come forward as she holds a sword in her right hand. Her stone throne has been carved with a cupid's face and butterflies. Atop her head is a golden crown with red embellishments and drapery. A single bird flies amongst the clouds in the background.

King
A man in light blue robes and grey cloak sits on a throne. This throne is embellished with butterflies and two crescent moons. He sits much taller than any of the surrounding trees. Two birds fly side-by-side amongst the clouds in the background.

The Wands Suit

The Wands Suit is considered interchangeable with the Clubs suit of a normal deck of cards.

Ace
A white hand comes from a thin grey cloud holding a staff or wand with leaves budding from the exterior. The hand hovers over a landscape with a river. In the distance is the silhouette of a building.

Two
A man faces off a terrace. He is adorned in orange with a red cloak and hat. In his left hand, he wields a staff/wand. In his right, he holds an orb with roses on the exterior. Another staff/wand stands upright behind him

Three

A man in red robes faces away from the viewer, looking over a barren desert with few mountains visible in the desert. He has a green cloth draped across his left shoulder and is holding a staff/wand in his right hand. Two staffs/wands stand upright behind him.

Four
A couple stands before a mass of people in the distance. They are walking away from a castle or similar building to four staffs/wands, standing upright from the ground. Draped across the staff is a length of greenery and fruit.

Five
Five well-dressed men stand in a circle. Each holds a wand/staff. There is nothing in the background beside a blue sky. The ground is barren with yellowing grass.

Six
A man adorned in a maroon cloak sits atop a green cloth draped across a white horse. The man holds a wand/staff with a wreath hanging from the top. In the background, men not on horses carry five extra wands/staffs.

Seven
A man holding a staff/wand stands atop a cliff. He is swinging the staff to protect himself from the six other staffs/wands extending from the base of the card.

Eight
Eight wands/staffs are angled from top left to the bottom right of the card. Though you cannot see the left ends, the right ends are not being held up by anything. In the background are a river and lonely hill with a house atop it.

Nine
A tired watchman wearing yellow tights and a red tunic leans against a staff/wand. The top of his head is bound in bandages. His eyes have draped closed as he stands watching over the eight staffs/wands behind him.

Ten

A man carries the ten wands/staffs he has gathered to the city in the distance. The environment is a barren desert.

Page
A fancily-dressed young man examines his wand/staff with great care. The landscape behind him is a group of sand dunes.

Knight
A knight in shining armor sits atop a brown horse. He is baring his wand/staff as the yellow, tattered cloth drapes from his torso. He has red plumage, not only on his head but also on his shoulder and elbow.

Queen
A lady adorned in a golden dress sits in an elaborate throne. She is holding her staff/wand in her right hand and a sunflower in her left. In front of her is a black cat.

King
The king is sitting in profile. He has red robes and an ornate cloak. He holds his wand/staff in his right hand. Beside his throne is a small lizard.

The Cups Suit

The Cups suit is comparable to the heart suit of a normal deck of cards.

Ace
The Holy Grail sits atop a white hand, extending from a grey cloud. A dove swoops from the heavens holding a coin embellished with the Hebrew letter Yod, to show divine intervention or guidance. From the cup, 5 streams of water overflow into the pond below. The pond is speckled with lily pads.

Two
A man and woman meet with each carrying a cup. The woman is wearing a white dress and a blue alb. The man is wearing an ornate golden tunic. Behind them is a caduceus, topped with a winged lion head.

Three
Three women form a circle, each raising a cup in celebration. Surrounding them is a large harvest. One woman has her back turned to the viewer. She is wearing a red cloak. The other two are wearing white dresses, though one has a leather tunic-like jacket.

Four
A hand, extending from a small grey cloud, holds out a cup for a man sitting at the base of a tree. The man is wearing a red undershirt and green tunic along with blue tights. He is sitting on the grass, ignoring the hand's cup in favor of choosing one of three other cups sitting before him.

Five
A figure cloaked in black looks down at 5 cups at his feet, three of which have been spilled. Across a river in the distance is a small town with a bridge connecting the two pieces of land.

Six
A young boy extends a white flower in a cup to a young girl. Around him are five more cups, each with a single white flower. They are in a town square. The boy is wearing a blue tunic with red tights and a hat. The girl is wearing a blue dress with a yellow coat. Around her head is a red scarf and on her hands are white gloves.

Seven
Sitting on a cloud, in front of a figure shrouded in darkness are seven cups, each has an item in it, representing one of the seven deadly sins. The first has a woman's face, representing lust and lustful thoughts to beautiful people. The second has a blanket, representing sloth and laziness. The third has a snake, representing the envious "snake in the grass". Cup number 4 has a castle, representing the gluttony of the feast inside. The fifth cup has a stack of gems and valuable treasures, symbolizing greed. The sixth cup has a laurel, a headpiece commonly seen in depictions of the Divine. It represents pride and vanity of putting oneself on equal footing with the Divine. The last cup has a wrathful, violent dragon. The shadowy figure could easily pass into heaven but instead spends his time focused on the contents of the cups, blocking him from his chance into paradise.

Eight
A man, adorned in a red robe, walks away from a river, away from eight cups stacked just over the river bend. He is rather elderly and carries with him a small staff. In the sky above, the moon looks down on him, lighting his way.

Nine
This card features a man in white robes and fancy red hat, sitting, arms crossed, on a wooden bench, looking at the viewer. Behind him, nine golden cups sit atop a shelf draped in a floor-length blue cloth.

Ten
A man stands with his arm around a woman. They both lift their free hands to the sky, gesturing to the rainbow of golden cups above them. The man wears a red tunic; the woman, a blue dress. A boy and a girl dance in a circle, holding hands. Their clothing mimics that of their parents.

Page
A young man in a fancy blue and pink tunic holds a cup in front of the ocean. His tunic is decorated with small flowers. Atop his head is a blue hat.

Knight
A knight in shining armor marches toward a river atop a grey horse. The plumes of his helmet are wing-shaped. With his hand, he holds a cup in front of him.

Queen
A woman in a white dress and golden crown holds an ornate chalice. She sits atop a wooden throne, embellished with cupids, that sits at the edge of a body of water. At her feet are small, round fruits and vegetables.

King
The king, wearing a blue robe with gold and red cape sits in a basic throne in the middle of an ocean. In one hand, he holds a scepter and in the other, a cup. On top of his head is a red crown and around his neck is a necklace with a large shell.

The Pentacles Suit

The Pentacles suit is equivalent to the Diamonds suit in a normal deck of cards.

Ace
A white hand, extending from a grey cloud, holds a large, golden pentacle in front of the exit to a garden. On either side of a path leading to the exit, there are several bell-shaped white flowers.

Two
A performer in red holds two golden pentacles inside an infinity sign. Behind him, two ships ride the waves of the ocean.

Three
Four women surround a man standing on a wooden bench, listening to what he has to say. They are all beneath a pillar, on top of which, four pentacles are carved into it.

Four
A person sits in front of a vast kingdom. They are in red robes with a black shawl and golden crown. Atop their head is a golden pentacle and in their arms is another. Beneath their feet are two more.

Five
Two homeless and tattered figures march barefoot through the snow in front of a church. The stained-glass window of this church has 5 golden pentacles as the core element of the design.

Six
A man in a blue tunic with red robes over top gives coins to a homeless person draped in a yellow blanket. Another homeless man sits to the other side, hands up for money, draped in a blue blanket. In addition to the money he is giving the first homeless person, the finely-dressed man is holding a scale, judging the worth of the homeless people. Around him are six golden pentacles, floating in the air.

Seven
A plain-dressed farmer leans against his trowel looking a bush. The bush sprouts six pentacles while a seventh lies at the man's feet.

Eight

A sculptor in a blue tunic, red tights, and black vest sits atop a wooden bench beside a tree. He is carving a pentacle onto a golden disc. In addition to the one he's finishing up, one pentacle lies on the ground beside him, one lies against the bench, and five are hung up on the tree beside him. He sits working in solitude, with only the tops of buildings visible in the distance.

Nine
A person stands before grape vines in a white robe with red flower designs and accents. On their left hand, they have a yellow glove, atop which sits a bird of prey. Amongst the grapes behind them are nine golden pentacles. Beyond that are two trees and the faint outline of a city.

Ten
Ten pentacles are scattered in the foreground of this card. They do not seem to be part of the scenery behind them. In that scenery, however, there is a lot going on. Two white dogs face an old woman, wrapped in a cloth depicting grape vines, and a carriage or other family heirloom. Behind her, a man in a grey tunic with a blue shawl speaks to a woman in a red dress with her child. The child is wearing a blue gown and is looking excitedly around his mother and at the dogs.

Page
A man in a green tunic looks at a pentacle he is holding in a lush green landscape. Atop his head is a fancy red hat. In the background, there is an edge of a forest to the viewer's left and a mountain to the right. In front of the mountain, but still far behind the man is a plot of farmland.

Knight
A knight in shining armor sits atop a black, long-haired horse. He holds a golden pentacle in front of him and is overlooking the farmland of the people he is sworn to protect. The horse's saddle bridle and tackle are a deep crimson, as is the tabard of the knight.

Queen
The queen's throne sits surrounded by wild flora and fauna. It is engraved with many creatures and plants. She is wearing a red gown with a green veil coming from her small crown. She is looking at a golden pentacle sitting in her lap. The top of the card is framed with vines and roses.

King
The king's throne sits just outside the city. His robes are made of grape vines and his crown is topped with three red roses. In one hand, he holds a golden scepter. In the other, he holds a golden pentacle.

CHAPTER 6
Cards Meanings

Many experienced divingers will recommend that once you have some experience, you come up with your own meanings for each symbol and aspect of each card. No two people will have exactly the same interpretation. This is due to the fact that these meaning will very from person to person because they will vary with the feelings you get from the cards and the energy you feel emanating from the card(s). No one person's interpretation of the cards and symbols is more valid than another's. It is about your energies, and your life and as such all the cards we be different for everyone. Some people may find that the recommended definitions and symbolic explanations that came with their deck are sufficient, which is perfectly acceptable.

Due to the difficulty and time required to define your terms for your Tarot Deck, almost all Tarot decks come with guides which will include pre set meanings and interpretations for the cards. While these may vary from deck to deck, they all follow similar trends and interpretations. This chapter will cover some of the most common pre-set meaning for each card, symbol, color, and number. This is in place of teaching you how to determine your own definitions. The reason for this decision is that given the intricate and deeply personal nature of Tarot cards and divining, it is not possible to construct a sufficient guide that would cover all aspects, and it is an art form, not so much a science. There is no algorithm for determining the meanings of cards, so here we have laid out the typical preset interpretations for Tarot cards. Once again, you may decide to keep some of these definitions, all, or even none of these definitions once you have some experience with divination. Whatever the case, that is okay, divination is a deeply personal journey, so there is no one size fits all. This will provide a useful starting point for definitions.

The vast majority of these cards have two meanings, and some have even more. Thoe with dual meanings are typically divided and determined via the orientation of the card when drawn. One definition will be for if it is drawn upright, and the other for when it is drawn reversed, or upside down. Some cards, however, have only one meaning regardless of orientation. In the following chapter, I will also lay out the symbolism of each card as I interpret it. This will include a master list of the symbols and what they may mean, then explain the symbolism to specific cards as they appear. This chapter will be structured the same way chapter 5, first listing the major arcana, followed by the minor arcana, then ordered by suit.

Symbolism

Colors

Red is used to represent dangers and sacrifice on the road ahead. Do not be distraught, for it represents passion and beauty as well. Be wary of the dangers ahead, because this color is also representative of anger and blood.

Pink represents womanhood, and the ideals associated with the feminine aspect of the divine. Some of these traits are tenderness, sensitivity, and romanticism. Alternatively, this color can be used to represent childhood and the associated traits such as curiosity, naivety, and an adventurous spirit.

Orange is representative of amusement and whimsy. It indicates something unusual lies ahead, which is often accompanied by adventure and possible danger. This is why it is not uncommon to see this color paired with red.

Yellow portrays both material and emotional wealth and happiness. As such, this color indicates an optimistic future with much worldly and emotional pleasure.

The color green often represents material money and prosperity. Additionally, it is deployed when fortelling growth and matters that pertain to nature, as well as being used to represent hope for the future.

While blue is often thought to represent sadness and serenity in literature, Tarot uses this interpretation as a mere bristle in its brush for painting the future; in Tarot, blue represents the whole range of emotions we may endure in our human experience. When used more positively, it represents peace, unity, and thoughtfulness.

Purple, while commonly representative of royalty in earth's history, also pertains to the psychic realm of emotions. Tied to this realm, it also represents the ability to solve problems and the logical reasoning capabilities of the user.

Beige in Tarot has a more linear interpretation in Tarot than the meaning it takes in most literature, as in most literature it represents flexibility, dependability, neutrality, and calmness. In Tarot, beige is thought to represent vulnerability, the opposite interpretation.

Brown represents earth, and often is used as an indicator that one should seek to ground their mental state, to taper being over zealous in your endeavors and expectations. When deployed in a descriptive fashion, it represents humility and subtlety.

Grey is often deployed in the context of mourning. In this context it portrays the wisdom and humility that loss often brings to bear. Staring down one's own mortality can be a humbling experience for almost anyone. But being faced with this mortality can often cause indecision, something to be avoided.

White is utmost example of purity, for it is the purity and balance that occurs when all the visible light spectrum is within a point, perfectly balanced. As such, when deployed in the context of Tarot, white represents perfection, innocence, and all that is good and honest in the world. This color is often deployed to indicate that you may have a clean start ahead of you, a new beginning with all its opportunities and possibilities. White is often used to show a lack of bias, as it is what we should all strive for.

Black is the most common color to appear in scenes and times of mourning. It is the antithesis to white. As white represents a new beginning and a clean slate, black often represents the toll of the bells of the final hours of some endeavor or existence. It can be used to represent violence, evil, and power, as what lurks in the darkness is often unknown, powerful, and, rarely, even violent and evil. The tie of black to finality leads to its status as a symbol for secrecy, as we mortals cannot be sure of what lies past our final hours on this earth.

Numbers

Zero is representative of infinite potential, it is the blank slate which white often leads to. It sits in the middle of all things, it gives the power to drift negativity, evil, and debt, but also the power to shift towards goodness, positivity, and wealth. In its state as a true balance, the potential yields from such a position are infinite.

One represents movement in the right direction from a new beginning. One indicates that the seeds of success have been planted, and the ground is fertile for new growth and that the plants grown shall be ripe with opportunity. Additionally, one is used to represent the masculine half of the Divine. This number is tied to the root chakra, which is vital for the grounding of oneself.

Two represents dualities and dichotomies. It represents a split in the path ahead, two distinct possibilities. These possibilities may be any combination of good or bad. There could be two good but separate paths, or one good and one bad, or even potentially two bad paths, this must be read in the context of its surrounding elements, symbols, and colors. Two is tied to the feminine half of the Divine. It is tied to the sacral chakra, which is important for changes in life.

Three represents that when two become one, the result is more than the sum of its parts. As the sum of the parts when two entities combine is two, and this number yields more than that. Additionally, it represents the two trinities at the core of all existence.
The first trinity is the triangle of mind, body, and spirit; the second trinity is composed of heaven, earth, and water. The number also signifies love and creation. Three is tied to the navel chakra, the chakra most used in the choices you must make in life.

The number four represents stability and structure. After all, this is the number of corners in most buildings, one could even infer that its significance as stability and structure is because the foundations of the cradle of civilization was often a quadrilateral.

This number also signifies discipline and being rooted/static. Being symbolic of stability, this number is tied to the heart chakra, which is responsible for balance and emotion.

The numeral five represents challenge and growth. More specifically, it represents the challenges one must face to grow, and the growth that results from overcoming adversity. It represents the combination of the four elements and the spirit, for these compose all of our reality, and our existence is one big challenge after another, with growth along the way. It is seen in the pentacel, five points, one for fire, earth, air, water, and of course, the spirit. Since it is often much easier to overcome adversity with communication and cooperation, this numeral is tied to the throat chakra. The throat chakra is used in communication endeavors.

Six represents success and suggests resting to recover from the struggle of the aforementioned number. It represents harmony and balance, which usually follow a successful struggle to grow. It is tied to the third eye chakra, which is important for perception.

The number seven is representative of forces beyond your control. These forces could be down to the actions of other people, natural creatures, weather, or even the divine. They are forces that will be unpredictable because they are beyond our control. They could aid you in your endeavors, or make them that much more treacherous to endure. These forces are often thought to be representative of the spirituality and wisdom within each of us, for although we may not understand them, it is our spirit and wisdom that will allow us to endure them unbroken. This number is tied to the crown chakra, which is the seat of knowledge in the chakri.

Eight represents an abundance of something. Largely what is being prophesied to be abundant is dependant on the other symbols present with this number, but it is usually beneficial to have an abundance of whatever it is the card refers to. It indicates that this abundance is brought about through your leadership, influence, honor, respect, as well as being a result of your power. As eight is closely tied to having more than you need, typically more than you will ever need, eight also symbolizes infinity.

The number nine represents completion of some task, as well as serving as a reminder to recollect on your past endeavors. It is important to reflect at the end of a struggle, in order to best learn and grow from such a struggle, so that the struggle wasn't for naught.
It reminds us to look back on not only our recent accomplishments, but our lives overall, and figure out how to incorporate our goals into the grand scheme of our lives. To make sure we are doing what is best, and to learn from our mistakes.

Of all the numbers in Tarot, ten represents more energy than any other. As such, it is the highest energy card in whatever suit it may be found. The satisfying, complete feeling we get from doing things in sets of ten has culminated in this number's symbolism as being the ultimate completion of some endeavor. This card indicates that your endeavors are either completed now, recently, or will be in the near future. Furthermore, this card indicates that after such a completion occurs, it is time to deem that chapter of your life completed. This opens the door for us to seek new projects and opportunities that we may not have otherwise sought, which will often lead to great wealth, both in spirit and material terms.

The Page is representative of youth. With this youth often comes news of new events (the youth doesn't necessarily mean a literal young person, often it just means something is younger and has more energy). This person, with their grounded demeanor and youth, are also representative of the earth.

The knights represent change and movement of ideas, people, and cultures. This is because of the campaigns that knights would classically take part in, bringing new ideas to different regions of the world. It is also because of these campaigns that these icons also represent youth and power. The knight is the foremost symbol of the power of a king, as they are to execute his will and support him in all endeavors. Knights were often younger and more fit than other members of their societies, as they had to travel far, train hard, and carry the weight of entire armies on their backs. Due to the moral codes which these knights abided by, they also represent purity of spirit, for they would do what they believed to be morally correct, even if it would lead to their doom.

The queens represent the peak of womanhood. These women serve not only as mothers to their children, but as a sort of maternal overseer for the entire kingdom. This was especially true when the king was off campaigning in foreign lands with his knights and warriors. Additionally, they served as advisors for their kings, and people who would help tame the fires in the king's heart, helping the king realize when he was mistaken, and how to turn his goals and ambitions into a reality. They are wise beyond their years, and often handled the more delicate matters of running a country. Their impeccable judgement allows them to tell when it is best to let the king handle things with fury and fire, as well as when to handle things more delicately. They are seen as symbols of maturity, and development. Additionally, they represent the element of water.

While queens represent the maternal, softer side of royalty and parentage, the king represents authority and unrivaled ambition. He is the force that forges the knights into the leaders and fighters that they are. Often ruling with maturity and a controlled fury, they are respected by most people, and considered some of the wisest in the land. Their fiery passions sometimes get the better of them, and that is where their queen comes into play, controlling the unbridled fury that the king would rain down upon his foes. Do not mistake this, the king is more than capable of handling himself in diplomatic matters, but much like a father to their children, he serves as the ultimate protector of his people. He is always on guard, watching for signs of danger and ready to respond at the drop of a hat.

Symbols

Angels are the messengers of the divine. These messengers may come to you in dreams or in the form of other people, be it friend, foe, or stranger.

Ankhs, much like their usage in Egypt, are used to represent eternal life. In Egypt, these symbols were often buried with the dead to signify that the short time they had on Earth was only a small portion of the eternal life that lay ahead.

Arches represent new paths and possibilities. This is because arches are most commonly found in place of doors or gates with a path going directly through the center.

Armor tells a story of preparation and protection. It shows the anticipation of challenges and willingness to fight for what you deem is right.

Benches represent rest and reflection.

Birds were commonly used as messengers and, as such, represent clear thought and communication. They can also be used to represent the element of air.

Blindfolds are self-explanatory. They represent not seeing clearly. This can be from ignorance or an outright denial of any part of the truth. However, blindfolds can also be seen as unbiased thoughts. In things such as justice, you weigh the situation without allowing your biases to change the outcome.

Boats represent, in simplest terms, relocation and change caused by emotion. The size of the ship can be used to represent the support network for any given change. They can also represent literal travel by sea.

Bridges represent the option to get out of the situation you are in. Given that water is most often representative of emotions, the bridge to get over it is allowing logic to supercede emotion to get you to a better situation.

Bulls represent Earth and the zodiac symbol of Taurus. They show strength and power. They are also a symbol of wealth and stock market growth.

Just as a butterfly starts as a caterpillar, the situations we are put through cause us to grow into beauty. Butterflies represent change. They represent letting go of the things that tie you down so you can be free and beautiful.

A Caduceus represent the god, Hermes and all things associated with him. These aspects include commerce, trade, and communication. It also represents balance as depicted by the symmetry of the design.

Castles are the physical manifestation of the goals we have set. They symbolize protection and civilization as well.

Cats are the epitome of grace and perception. A cat can also be used to represent psychic knowledge.

Chains are limitations or restrictions that prevent us from achieving our goals. These may never be visible to us, but are restrictions nonetheless.

Circles are symbols of perfect infinity. They represent completion. They are used to represent cycles and things with no beginning and no end.

Much like the common children's game of deciphering images from clouds, clouds are symbols of clear thoughts and sudden epiphanies, like when you can finally see the image above.

Crayfish/lobsters represent cyclical changes as they commonly shed their shells. They represent the mystery of emotion as they climb from the watery depths.

Crosses are used to represent the union of spirit and body. The four points both symbolize the four elements and the cardinal directions.

Crowns represent Divine-given power and the relationship those in power have with the Divine. It expertly combines physical and spiritual conversation.

A cup represents femininity and water. The exact meaning of a cup depends on what is inside.

Deserts represent fire. They can also represent a harsh apathy.

Dogs represent the physical realm and civilized people. They are domesticated companions and provide protection. Dogs are said to provide ample protection to the soul in the spirit realm.

The dove represents peace, purity, and untainted love. They are commonly used to represent the grace and kindness of the divine.

Dragons simply represent power or dominion over others. It may also suggest a hoard of worldly pleasure, such as the gold collection commonly depicted in a dragon's lair.

Eagles are representative of air. It shows the aspects of the mind and intelligence. They represent power and use their authority to spread truth. As they eat serpents, they also commonly are used to represent God.

Feathers, much like the birds from which they are from, represent air and connection to the spirit realm. As a quill, they represent communication and expression of thoughts.

Fish obviously represent water, but also represents the unconscious mind and your emotions. They are said to bring messages from the unconscious mind to light.

Flags represent announcements and the arrival of news or something that is not material in nature. News introduced with a flag are generally major changes or important information.

Flames represent the dichotomy of creation and destruction. The sun, a ball of flaming gas, brings life, but if a fire is not tended to, it will wreak havoc on the environment. They can also represent purification and the destruction of anything corrupt. Creation is not always positive, as bombs or explosions created with the element cause more harm than good. Likewise, destruction is not always negative, as in the grassland, grass fires are common and a natural and necessary part of the survival of that ecosystem.

Flowers represent beauty and growth. They also represent the creative process.

Fruits and vegetables represent the harvest and the rewards that can be reaped from hard work and great effort.

Gardens represent growth and abundance of resources. They represent the seeds of success you plant early in the seasons of life in order to reap the reward as it comes to fruition. They can also be used to represent creativity and beauty.

Grapes represent luxury and pleasure, as they are used to make wine. Grapevines, however, represent ambition and effort because they grow up to the sun the same way our ambitions grow up toward our goals, latching on to things to help it on its journey. It is not a pest to the things it uses to further its goal, rather it adds beauty and, in some cases, even protects the things it uses.

Hammers represent physical labor and the success that comes through it. However, one must be careful. If physical labor takes priority over your personal health, one can only expect pain in the long run.

Hands represent the dichotomy of giving and receiving. When disembodied, they show Divine intervention and the actions they are doing become imperative to the card's meaning.

The heart combines the mind or emotions and the body to the spiritual realm. Many people think the heart is where the Divine resides within a person. More obvious is the representation of love and kindness.

Horses represent movement and strength. It is said that the horse represents the raw energy of human ambition. A wild horse shows untamed potential that, by reigning in and controlling, can be a major asset in your journey to achieve your hopes and dreams.

Infinity represents the beginning and the end, the combination of energy and physical attributes, and how you can never hope to separate any one aspect of life from the rest. Simply put, infinity represents how everything intertwines.

An iris represents faith and courage, hope and wisdom. The flower also represents the clear communication of ideas.

Jewels represent success and the ability to splurge. However, it should be noted that, if not managed carefully, can lead to a materialistic viewpoint in which one can never be truly happy or at peace.

Keys are symbols of answers and learned knowledge as they unlock the doors that hide information.

Lamps represent intellectual enlightenment and clarity. They can also be a beacon of hope in dark times.

Laurels represent victory and successful campaigns.

Leaves, like gardens, show growth and health.

Lightning shows sudden Divine interference. Like fire, lightning harnesses the dichotomy of creation and destruction.

Lilies are a symbol of purity and innocence. However, they are also used to represent fertility and maternal figures. It symbolizes femininity and the feminine portion of the Divine.

Lions represent kings and emperors. They show strength and pride. They are commonly associated with fire.

The moon represents the feminine Divine. It represents our emotions and is a reflection of our experiences brought forth to physical manifestation. They also represent cycles and the constant process of ending and beginning again.

Mountains are used to represent challenges, the ups and downs of life. With proper growth, you can overcome it, though it is important to recognize the risk involved.

Nudity shows that you are open and willing to listen to the message given to you. It can sometimes represent sexuality.

The ocean represents our subconscious mind, both when calm and story. It can also be a symbol of the vast mysteries surrounding our existence and the very universe we live in.

Olive branches are a common symbol of peace. They are often seen in the beak of a dove flying down from the heavens.

Palm branches represent success and victories over those who go against us.

Paths represent our path in life. They may lead to self-discovery and the path of spiritual guidance.

Pentacles are used to represent earth. Some people call them "coins" because they represent money and material wealth. They also represent stability, security, and nature itself.

Pillars represent balance and grounding. When two frame the card, it represents neutrality and the middle-ground.

Pomegranates represent fertility and the female sexuality.

A pool of water is associated with the moon and emotions. It is also commonly tied to being made clean.

Pyramids represent personal development and using manpower to create something great and long lasting.

Rabbits represent the Earth as well as family and fertility. They are fast and sensitive, making good decisions quickly.

Rainbows symbolize femininity and peace. They can also represent intellectual enlightenment

The ram represents action and bravery. They are responsible and determined, often seeming hardheaded or arrogant.

The river represents changing emotion. As the water ebbs and flows, so too does our emotional wellbeing.

Roses can represent life, love, and passion. It is, surprisingly, a representation of masculinity and is also said to represent purity of spirit.

Salamanders represent fire. They are nocturnal and bask in the sun during the day. Thy are a symbol of renewal based on their ability to regrow their tails and adaptability due to their ability to lose them in the first place.

Scales represent balance and justice. They show the truth by weighing the options.

Scrolls represent knowledge and wisdom kept secret. An unraveled scroll shows the sharing of this information and the opening of the heart to those around you.

Snails represent self-reliance given they carry their homes on their backs. They also represent that sometimes, to achieve results, you have to take things slowly, one step at a time.

Snakes are commonly used to represent the devil. They are cunning and wise, yet cautious. The both represent male sexuality and female power.

Snow represents a challenge to survive but is a symbol of purity and restorative rest.

Spheres represent perfect completion. They also represent the Earth.

Sphinxes represent the mysteries of life, both good and bad.

A staff is included to represent stability and support. It symbolizes focus on a single point or aspect.

Stained glass is meant to remind us to look at things from afar, seeing things as a whole, rather than their individual parts.

Stars are symbols of hope. As the wise men followed the north star in the story of Jesus's birth, stars represent guidance and as many children are raised to understand, stars represent wishes.

The sun symbolizes life, as nothing could live without it. It is a symbol of masculinity and clarity of thought. It represents your ego and who you are at your deepest level.

Sunflowers represent all things happy and optimistic.

Swords represent honor and virtue and air. It represents the communication and the thoughts and actions of the mind.

The throne represents authority and support.

A tomb is used to represent the rest before being reborn or brought to a place of eternal life.

Towers represent connection between your conscious thoughts and the Divine. They are either strong and sturdy, or easily crumbled, representing your state of mind.

Towns represent civilization and teamwork, commerce and abundance.

Triangles are symbols of love and the combination of two parts into one new whole.

Trumpets are commonly symbols of the importance of a message.

A veil represents what is hidden or subconscious. It represents that which is not easily seen.

The symbol of Venus is representative of the goddess, Aphrodite as well as all attributed to her, such as womanhood and beauty.

A wall can show protection and safety but can just as easily be used to hide what you do not wish to acknowledge.

Wands represent fire, passion, drive, and desire. They are the lifeblood of everything and represent the bridge between the mind, body, and spirit.

Wheat symbolizes fertility and the goddess Demeter, and all attributed to her, such as the harvest and abundance.

Wings are symbolic of flight, literal or otherwise. They show a communication channel to the Divine. Two wings together represent dichotomies, harmony, and balance.

Wolves are undomesticated and represent our animal instincts. They can be frightening yet beautiful and mysterious. They are also lone creatures, representing self-sufficiency.

Yod is the tenth letter in the Hebrew alphabet and represents the Divine and their presence in our lives.

Major Arcana

0 The Fool

When this card is drawn upright, it can mean the beginning or change that leads to adventure or personal growth. However, this adventure is not necessarily good, and you need to really think about the choice, as the Fool also represents recklessness. Trust your instincts but know when your mind needs to take the wheel.

If you draw this card in reverse, watch out. Reckless behavior can lead to bad decisions if you are not careful. Perhaps you need to reevaluate a choice or plan you have made. Make sure it is truly the best decision for you.

Symbolism:

First and foremost, the fool is represented by the number 0. This shows that the fool, lacking any proper knowledge, has the potential to learn and become anything. Next, you may notice the white dog at the bottom of the card. Dogs are a symbol of protection, and this dog is protecting the fool from his own ignorance and naivety. In the background of the card, you see the sun, showing that the fool is carefree and full of life. Despite his ignorance, a staff is included to show that the fool has at least a little stability in life. He is ignoring his challenges, represented by the mountains in the background, as he looks to the future. Finally, in his hand is a white rose to represent the childlike purity of his spirit.

In terms of color association, the predominant colors are yellow, representing his optimism, and orange, representing his amusement with life and the possible danger lurking around the corners due to his ignorance.

I The Magician
The Magician represents original ideas and actions. If you draw this card upright, you should take quick action on the things you've been stalling on. You need to be active in your life and not passively watch it pass you by.

If this card is drawn in reverse, you may be controlled by your ego or greed. Take time to reevaluate your life and your priorities and perhaps loosen up a bit.

Symbolism:
The magician is represented by the number one. This suggests that not only is he well grounded in spirit, but he also has room to grow and expand. It suggests that he has planted a seed to be reaped later in life.

On his card, he has one of each of the minor arcana suits, representing balance and harmony as well as the four elements, a cup for water, a wand for fire, a sword for air, and a pentacle for earth. Above his head is an infinity sign pointing to the idea that he is both the beginning and the end. It, along with the suit symbols, show how everything intertwines into perfect harmony. He also has both a rose, showing his passion and love for his craft, and a lily, showcasing his unity with the divine.

Much of the card is yellow, showing an optimistic future, full of wealth, happiness, and pleasure. His robe is red, showing his passion for his art, and his white tunic shows the neutrality and purity he resonates.

II The High Priestess
If this card is drawn upright, you have hidden knowledge about a choice you must make or an action you must take. Trust your instincts and listen to your subconscious mind. It knows what to do, or at the very least, what not to do.

If drawn in reverse, this card says to take action. Do not waste any more time thinking about possible outcomes. You know what you must do and you need to quit stalling.

Symbolism:
The entirety of this card represents duality. The first, most obvious case of this is that the high priestess is represented by the number two. This number, also represents the feminine aspects of the divine. Another clear case of this is the use of colors. The pillars are one each of black and white, the negative and the positive, the absence and presence of something. In addition to those two colors, another prominent one would be that of blue, showing the harmony between the dichotomies laid out on the card. In addition, crosses are said to represent the unity of the spirit and the body, and pillars represent balance.

Other symbols on the card are the pomegranate and moon, both of which represent the femininity of the card, a crown to show authority, and a veil and scroll, both representing knowledge kept hidden. Finally, she sits atop a bench to show that she has taken a step back to reflect on the events that have happened in her life.

III The Empress

When drawn upright, this card suggests that you need to grow closer with the natural world. It promises success, fertility, and a happy home life, but only once you realize the prerequisite is a generous and loving personality.

The reversed rotation of the card suggests that maybe you are splurging too much, too often. Make sure to not let greed cause depression and a loss of energy.

Symbolism:
The empress is represented by the number 3, showing the love and creativity of a maternal figure such as herself. This idea is further supported by the appearance of her heart shield, wheat, and leaves. Her femininity is also shown by the symbol of venus and the pomegranate speckling her dress. Her power as a mother is represented by her crown of stars. The stars represent the hope of her children's growth under her order.

The optimism of this card is shown in the mass amounts of yellow used. Other colors included on the card are the red of passions of passion and the greens of growth and hope.

IV The Emperor
The upright Emperor represents power and authority, as well as discipline. When making a decision, make sure you are not basing it solely on emotion, but on a strong, logical foundation. It also represents authority, meaning if you are facing a problem, you will be able to face it alone with proper planning.

Simply put, a reversed Emperor represents an abuse of power. It shows plans that are falling apart and are in need of repair. When making decisions, be realistic and do not ask too much of any one person, or even yourself.

Symbolism:
The emperor is the 4th card of the Major Arcana. This number represents stability and discipline, setting out the emperor as a paternal figure. His power is shown through, not only his crown, but also the ram heads on his throne and even the throne itself. While the mountains in the background show possible struggles looming, the emperor is prepared, baring his armor. The ankh in one hand represents eternal life, while the sphere in the other represents a completion.

The main color of this card is red, symbolising his passion and the possible danger and sacrifice looming behind him.

V The Hierophant
This card in the upright position represents the study of tradition and, not only states that tradition works, but asks you to study and find out *why* it works and how that can be adapted. Follow tradition but open your mind to new possibilities.

Upside down, this card can be as simple as just telling you that someone is lying to you. It can also be representative of rebellions without cause.

Symbolism:

The 5 that represents the Hierophant also represents the idea of the challenges we must go through in order to grow. It also represents the harmony of the four elements with the spirit, as does the cross topping his staff. The cross and crown also represent the harmony of mind, body, and spirit. The pillars framing the card put the hierophant in the middle ground, and given that the throne provides authority to those who sit upon it and the staff shows focus, the keys at his feet are the answers he is willing to provide.

Colors associated with this card are, first and foremost, the red of passion and beauty. The yellows of the crown and staff hint at optimism and pleasure. The greys of his pillars further show his wisdom.

VI The Lovers
Upright, this card most obviously represents love. Whether this is the love of an object or of a person, this love is potent and powerful. You may complete a goal in pursuit of this love, or you may find yourself with a new opportunity to let this love flourish.

Reversed, this card represents letting go. You cannot move on until you've broken ties with the things that have hurt you. Let the unhealthy loves of your life leave to allow yourself to progress.

Symbolism:
The number 6 represents balance and suggests that you deserve a break because of your success. The angel is a bringer of news, presumably good news as shown by the sun behind them and based on the nudity of the lovers, they are open to hearing that news, while the cloud shows a sort of epiphany. The snake, however, when tied with the nudity, represents the sexuality of the lovers. The mountain in the background show the ups and downs of a relationship and the flames show the result, whether that be creation or destruction.

Colors associated with this card are the yellow optimism of love and the beige vulnerability of being in a relationship.

VII The Chariot

Upright, this card states that with a controlled ego and self-discipline, nothing is unattainable. Be optimistic and authoritative but do not abuse your power. Any conflict you are currently facing, you will emerge victorious with discipline.

When reversed, this card simply states that sheer force doesn't always solve problems. Perhaps you need to look at things in a new light and find a non-violent solution. Discouragement may be keeping you from completing a task or attaining a goal you have set. When you look at yourself in a position of power, are you a bully or hard-headed, or are you open-minded and compassionate?

Symbolism:
The number 7 represents wisdom or things beyond our control. These may be mysterious or puzzling to use as shown by the sphinxes, the colors showing both the good and bad in these mysteries. There are also many symbols of power and protection, such as the crown, staff, armor, and castle. The moon, star, and river represents our hopes, dreams, and emotions. However, the inclusion of the laurel on the charioteer's head shows eventual victory.

Other colors of this card are the yellow of emotional pleasure, wealth, and happiness and the blue of emotions and thoughtfulness.

VIII Strength
This card, when drawn upright, represents, as you've probably already guessed, strength. However, instead of referring just to pure brute strength, it also references willpower and standing strong under pressure. Your health may be improving or maybe you are just able to give up an unhealthy lifestyle.

When drawn in reverse, this card warns if you do not keep hold of your pride and impulses, you are at risk of losing control or becoming wrathful.

Symbolism:
This card is represented by the number 8, showing abundance and leadership. It can also be used to represent the infinity shown on the card. Infinity represents the idea of beginnings, ends, and

cycles. It shows us that everything intertwines in some way. Other symbols on this card are the lion, showing strength, and the flowers, representing growth and the creative process.. Having the lion's jaw forced closed tells us to repress our pride when it starts becoming a problem.

Colors associated with this card are yellow, showing worldly and emotional pleasure that comes with not only strength of body, but strength of will, the orange of possible danger if we allow things to get out of hand, and the green of prosperity, hope, and growth.

IX The Hermit
Upright, this card suggests taking a step back, away from everyone else, and take a moment of solitude. In this solitude, you may find answers you never knew you had. It can also represent balance and harmony in the middle of chaos.

Though upright, it means to disconnect from others, when this card is reversed, it may mean you have disconnected from yourself. Do not be impatient, listen to your inner guide, and listen to the advice of others around you.

Symbolism:
The number nine paired with the solitude of the hermit represent taking a step back to recollect your thoughts. The staff represents stability and wisdom during this time, while the fallen snow represents rest. Additionally, the lamp represents the enlightenment that will come from this time spent in solitude.

Colors associated with this card are the blue of thoughtfulness, the grey of wisdom, and white for the purity of results.

X Wheel of Fortune
Generally, there is only one meaning for this card, whether you drew it upright or reversed. It is a good card overall. This card brings word of good luck and the answers to your struggles, even if it is just to saddle up for the ride and wait for it to pass. For this to come across, however, you must be willing to broaden your perspective and see things from another point of view. Make sure, even in the change of fate, to maintain balance.

Symbolism:
This card is represented by both the numbers 1 and 10. 1 is the seed of success and through these seeds you may ground yourself; 10 represents energy and completion. The bull and lion represents strength and power; the sphinx alludes to the mysteries of life, this sphinx holds a sword in its hands alluding to the thoughts and actions of the mind. The snake and eagle represent wisdom. All of these symbols sit atop a cloud. This platform represents these ideas coming to light.

The red of this card represents the danger and beauty, sacrifice and passion of life. The orange represents the adventures you will face and the yellow represents the potential lens of optimism in which we can view all aspects of life through.

XI Justice

As you might expect, this card, at least in its upright position, represents fairness and unbiased equality. This may not be a good thing though. For example, if you know you've done something wrong, it may be time to accept the consequences of those actions.

Reversed, this card means just the opposite. It represents injustice and inequality. This injustice could have been served to you or from you. It depends entirely on the circumstances of the draw. Make sure to not blame others for your own shortcomings and take responsibility for your actions.

Symbolism:
Justice is represented by the number two as there are generally two options in true justice, guilty and innocent, right and wrong. The idea of true justice is further supported by the framing of the card with pillars, showing the person as a neutral entity, free of bias. There is a sword of honor and a scale to weigh the options and pass judgement. The judge sits atop a bench to reflect on the situation at hand, the veil behind him obscuring things that may give a bias.

Colors associated with this card are the red of sacrifice, the yellow optimism hiding behind the veil, and the purple to represent logic and problem solving needed to fairly judge someone.

XII The Hanged Man
The upright orientation of this card represents martyrdom and self-sacrifice. This doesn't necessarily mean death, but maybe you need to give up some emotional or material things that you have grown attached to for the betterment of those involved and those around you.

If reversed, someone need a shift of paradigm. Look at your situation from a new angle and you may be in for a shock. Look at the things and attachments you are involved with in this new light. It may be time to let some of them go.

Symbolism:
This card is represented by the number 3, which showcases the connection between heaven and earth. It also shows the love and creation associated with said connection. The cross the man is hanging from represents the union of body and spirit. The blue of the background shows thoughtfulness and the grey mixed in shows wisdom. This leads to eventual growth, shown by the leaves. The red suggests a possible sacrifice but also potential beauty.

XIII Death
Though this card almost always is drawn to warn or tell of a major life change, that change is very rarely literal death. The upright orientation tells you that if there is a sudden change in your life, go with it and trust in the guidance of the cards. As the saying goes, when one door closes, another door opens. This card simply signifies that proverb.

Reversed, this card warns of the possible horror and dread attached to change. You may want to be stagnate in your situation, but change is for the best. New ideas can help give you a push to the change you need. Cut out the unused items in your life and allow this change to take place.

Symbolism:
Death is represented by the number 4, showing the unification of mind, body, and spirit. It also shows love and kindness, despite what the card may be interpreted as. The idea of love is emphasised by the inclusion of roses in the imagery. Death himself is wearing armor and riding a horse to show that he is strong and prepared for

what lies ahead. The boat in the background, when paired with the flag death is carrying, shows that he brings news of a change in cycle or direction. The tower and crown both show power.

The black and white together show a dichotomy of beginnings and ends and represent the cycles of change. The yellow goes to show that the change may be what is best in a given situation.

XIV The Temperance
This card, drawn upright, suggests that the easiest way to solve a problem may be to look at it logically. Perhaps you are being too emotional and that is clouding your judgement. Take a breather, meditate if you need to, and think before you act. Temperance brings together things that are otherwise opposites. Bring together your emotional spirit and the logical matter of your problem. Experience new things but maintain your security and safety.

Also suggesting you may not have thought things through, this card, when reversed, suggests you may not have planned things out as much as needed. You've lost control of the situation and may be becoming impatient and angry as a result.

Symbolism:
5 represents this card, telling the tale of a challenge to overcome. Out path goes directly through mountains of challenge but that doesn't mean we should cease travel because just past them lays the yellow sun of success and pleasure. The Angelic messenger brings cups filled with cleansing water. On her chest is a triangle to show love and in the reeds behind her are irises of hope, courage, and wisdom.

Besides yellow, some other colors that represent this card are the perfect, untainted white of a new beginning, the pink of motherly tenderness, and the blue of serenity. Green is also used to show growth and hope.

XV The Devil
Despite the Devil being the epitome of evil in most religions, this card, when upright, is very positive. It represents willpower and commitment. It also shows persistence and permanence. This card

is especially good if you are asking about a workplace problem or if you need help getting things done.

Reversed, however, this card represents weakness of mind, body, and soul. You may be trapped by an attachment you just can't let go. You may also be plagued with greed, anger, lust, or ignorance. It also represents our animalistic instincts. Bad connotation aside, it can be good if drawn where one needs commitment to succeed.

Symbolism:
The devil is represented by 6, showing balance and success. Above his head is a star to show hope and guidance. The couple before him are nude and open to hear what he has to say. Each has a tail; the man's tail is made of the flames of life and the woman's is made of the grapes of luxury. They are restricted by chains

The background is black to not only the power of life but also the finality of relying heavily on worldly pleasures. The Beige of the card shows our vulnerability to said pleasures.

XVI The Tower
This card, when positioned upright, represents a necessary change. Like Death, it states that this change will be sudden. This may include tearing down misconceptions or receiving flashes of insight. Do not fear this change, however, as it may just be a good thing in disguise.

When drawn in the reversed position, this card signifies sudden disaster and emotional turmoil. You must be logically minded in this sea of change, as emotionally driven dreams and fantasies will not help. Do not pretend you are secure. Make sure you are truly safe in this change because it will come one way or the other. Simply put, saddle up and ride it out.

Symbolism:
This card is represented by 7 which alludes to the divine. The idea of divine intervention is littered throughout this car. The crown and tower both represent a connection with the divine and, given both have been toppled, a weak connection can be assumed. The lightning and appearance of Yod as rain show divine intervention.

Black shows the power of the influence while yellow shows the intention of such, as this color represents happiness and pleasure. Grey shows the wisdom of the divine in the clouds as well as the indecision of those in power, represented by the ruined tower. Finally, red shows the danger of failing to abide by the will of the Divine.

XVII The Star
Though not providing a solution to a problem, this card, in its upright position, represents a good chance you will overcome the problem at hand. It represents hope, inner wisdom, and awareness both emotional and spiritual. It also represents artistic endeavors and a healthy life.

When drawn in reverse, the card represents self-doubt and pessimism. It tells of rejected opportunities that should have been taken up.

Symbolism:
The star has 8 points, showing leadership, influence, and how things intertwine. Each star represents hopes and wishes while the nudity of the lady shows an open mind towards life. She holds two cups of cleansing water, watering the gardens of growth. The mountains of challenge are four in the distance. The bird between the woman and her challenges represents clear thought.

The largest yellow star shows optimistic wishes and the greenery surrounding the woman gives us hope that the wishes will come to fruition with the thoughtfulness as represented by the blue water. The Beige color of the woman tied with her nudity shows her vulnerability to circumstance.

XVIII The Moon
The upright position of this card signifies creativity and new ideas. It shows unexpected results and, as such, should be combined with an air of caution. This card, in this position, can also signify negative aspects, such as confusion, fear, and lies.

Reversed, this card brings many negative interpretations with it. A secret about yourself may be uncovered, you may be dealing with emotional problems due to your subconscious surfacing and becoming conscious thoughts, or you may just be having problems sleeping.

Symbolism:
This card is represented by the rest and reflection of the number 9. The towers framing the card and the replacement of the stars with Yod show divine connection. The canines show the dichotomy of our nature; the dog is domestic, civil even while the wolf is driven by instinct, it is primal in nature. Both aspects are looking to the divine for guidance, represented by the mixture of a sun and moon in the sky. Out from the blue waters of emotion, a logical, purple lobster of change climbs onto a path. This is the path of life, which goes unavoidably through mountains of challenges, lined on the other side with hopeful greenery. All instances of the divine or their influences are an optimistic yellow.

XIX The Sun

Upright, this card is considered to be one of the best Tarot cards foretelling success. It has almost nothing but positive interpretations, including solving a problem and happy days.

Some of the negative or reversed meanings of this card include an inflated ego, misjudgment or delay that keep the problem from being solved.

Symbolism:
The sun shows a new beginning and a clean slate. This idea is further expounded upon by the number 1 representing this card. 0 also represents this card, and it is tied with the image of a child, suggesting the infinite potential when provided with a new day. A protective wall preserves the innocence of the nude, open minded child. The beige vulnerability is clearly shown and a horse mount represents the boundless energy of the child. The red flag tells us of the beauty of childish naivety while also warning of the danger of such a mindset. The sunflowers, both in the background and around the child's head brags of happiness and optimism brought by protection and ignorance.

XX Judgement

This card tells of sudden change, most often change we find scary or actively avoid. The outcome of this change depends on how you approach it. With courage and authority, you will succeed. However, with cowardice, success will be hard to come by.

Symbolism:
Judgement is represented by the dualistic nature of 2, in this case, innocent vs guilty, and the potential of 0. The angel their trumpet and their flag all bring news as the dead are reborn from their tombs. The reborn are naked and open to hearing the clarity that sits atop the wise, grey clouds. The mountains set against the peaceful blue sky show the challenges to faith overcome to reap the rewards.

XXI The World
The upright orientation of the World represents completion and wholeness. Perhaps you've been promoted to a higher position of power or graduated from a school of thought. Maybe you've gained deeper understanding about a topic. In any case, this is a great card for readings of the future or success.

When drawn in reverse, this card, simply put, states you reap what you sow. If you are unwilling to put effort into things and remain stagnant in your position, you cannot expect to grow. The same can be said if you try to reap harvest before it is ready. If you are impatient and cannot wait for the situation to flourish with fruit of success, you will not receive any success.

Symbolism:
The world represents the unity of mind, body, and spirit as shown by the association with 3. The nude figure in the center is adorned with a laurel of victory, brought about by her wands of drive, purple sash of logic, and overall open mindedness. She hovers in the middle of a cyclical circle surrounded by 4 creatures – an eagle of truth, a bull of power, a lion of pride, and an angel of the divine- which has assisted in her eventual victory
Other colors associated with this card are a peaceful blue, a vulnerable beige, and a hopeful and prosperous green.

Minor Arcana
The Swords Suit

Swords represent air and the honor and virtue associated with the element. They represent our thoughts and actions and how they intersect. All cards of this suit will cover these topics in some way.

Ace
Upright, you lead the charge to victory with clear thought and the ability to see through deception. With this card comes new beginnings, power, and positive change.

Reversed, it suggests you may try to lead through tyranny and raw power. The delusions of doing the right thing ultimately lead to embarrassment and a misuse of power.

Symbolism:
The ace of swords presents us with the idea of growing honor. The crown, appearance of Yod multiple times, and disembodied hand giving us the sword can be used to verify this. The mountains in the background tell of challenges to come while the palm and olive branches suggest victory through peace.

Colors associated with this card are the white of beginnings, the blue of unity and peace, and the yellow of optimism.

Two
Upright, this card brings ideas of a resolved disagreement. It synthesizes the differences into balanced harmony. If you've been in a disagreement with a person, this card may represent a true compromise where no one is given the short end of the stick.

The reversed orientation represents a stalemate. This may be brought about by each party being arrogant, or just by indecision. It also suggests you may be running away from the problem at hand or are misrepresenting something.

Symbolism:
The 2 of swords list possible dichotomies that may aid or disrupt the achievement of your goals. While the ocean and blindfold suggest mystery and ignorance, the cloud looming over the mountain of struggle suggest clarity of thought. While the blues represent sadness, the yellows represent happiness and optimism.

The moon represents cycles of ends and beginnings and the grey dress represents indecision.

Three
This card is not the best to draw, as the imagery may suggest. Upright, it represents bad times and hurt feelings leading to a hurting heart, but also suggests a deeper understanding of the problem at hand.

Reversed, this card represents sorrow, confusion, and betrayal that leads to heartbreak. It may also suggest loneliness or that someone is avoiding resolution to a problem.

Symbolism:
The 3 of swords suggests creation through unity of honor, virtue, and our thoughts. The heart represents the mind, body, and soul; the swords piercing it are the traits listed above being combined with the aspects of self. The clouds on a white background represent wise, clear thoughts.

Four
This card, when drawn upright, represents withdrawal and meditation leading to recovery and replenishment. Perhaps, you need to take a step back from those around you and spend time fixing yourself.

Reversed, it suggests you may be restless or just completely deny the state you are currently in. It states you may be taking action but are achieving no result.

Symbolism:
The 4 of swords represents the discipline of mind, body, and spirit through virtue and honor. The stained glass over the tomb reminds us to rest and look at the big picture. The wisdom of grey and optimism of yellow resonate throughout this card.

Five
This card, when upright, simply means defeat or backing away from a position. This could be for you or for someone else. It depends completely on the context of the draw.

Drawing the card in reverse suggests you may have someone plotting to stab you in the back. It represents treachery and spite, and a situation where there is ultimately no winner. It also suggests you may be winning the battle, but you've lost the war. It suggests weakness, humiliation, degradation, and indecision, while also suggesting there may be selfish motives involved.

Symbolism:
The 5 of swords represents the challenges we may face while attempting to be honorable. The clouds over the ocean represent the realisation that we can never fully know what to expect on the journey other than the mountainous challenges in our path.

Colors associated with this card are blue, showing thoughtfulness and possible sadness, grey, showing indecision, red, representing the idea that the result could be dangerous or beautiful or both, and green, representing the hope we have of prosperity and growth.

Six
Just as the shrouded figures seek refuge across the water, this card, when drawn upright, represents the journey in which you leave the pain behind to recover. However, it doesn't mean you have to take this journey alone. This card suggests you get support from those you can trust, as it will help build a brighter future for you.

When reversed, this card represents cowardice. You are running away from your problems instead of facing it head on. Your procrastination only delays the inevitable.

Symbolism:
The 6 of swords suggests we may need a break to truly achieve honor. While the ocean is a mystery, the boat is a form of stability and support as we cross. The blue ocean can be full of emotion, but the wise grey of the swords' honor helps us on our journey to prosperity represented by the yellow sky.

Seven
The upright position suggests everything comes with due diligence. Coming up with ideas outside the realm of what's considered normal or usual will lead to a partial success with confidence.

Much in the way of the man sneaking away from camp with the weapons, drawing this card in reverse signifies action without honor, deceit, or even a literal theft. It shows betrayal and deception, as if someone is preparing to stab you in the back.

Symbolism:
The 7 of swords represent divine gifts because of thoughts and actions and the possibility of losing them. The yellow, when paired with red, represents the dangers of relying too heavily on worldly pleasures.

Eight
You are powerless and trapped in the situation. You past may come to haunt you and throw you into a depression due to the restrictions placed on you. This card can also represent being censored or an oncoming crisis.

Symbolism:
The 8 of swords shows the influence honor and virtue can bring. The blindfold and clouds show two possibilities of influence, the blindfold being ignorance and denial and the clouds being clarity. The castle on the mountain represents the protection and power that can be brought about by this influence and the calm, blue pool of water offering cleansing and another chance at honor. The red dress represents the danger that can come from examining only past examples of virtue rather than looking at the current situation.

Nine
This card can represent regret and shame, but can also represent suspicion, especially that of infidelity. It can also suggest anxiety and a feeling of hopelessness.

Symbolism:
The 9 of swords represent the completion of life that comes with being honorable. The rose blanket with blue patches represent the peace and unity of life. The black background gives an air of power.

Ten
When drawn in either position, the solemn messages of this card ring clear. It tells of sudden, lasting bad luck. It foretells of ruin and anguish, betrayal and failed dreams. Most of all, it tells of disappointment.

Symbolism:
The 10 of swords represent the energies that come from our thoughts and actions, be it for better or worse. The sun, representing peace and happiness, can be seen vaguely over the mountains of struggle. The black sky with the ocean below represents a secrecy and mystery in life. The red warns of the dangers of the consequences of your actions.

Page
This card, while upright, represents dexterity and vigilance. Be ready and willing to negotiate and always be willing to gain new knowledge. This card also represents subtlety.

Representing the deviousness of people, the reversed orientation suggests that they too are ever vigilant, but in a manner of deceit, haste, and gossip. Perhaps someone is involved in a secret; perhaps you, yourself are this person. Be critical, but not overly so. This card generally brings bad news.
Number Associations:
The Page represents youth and earth. They are often used to announce the arrival of news.

Symbolism:
The page of swords claim that with honor and virtue, comes longevity. The clouds and birds show clear communication with the mountains in the background barely visible. The blue sky brings peace and thoughtfulness while the grey sword brings the wisdom that stands beside honor.

Knight
This card, upright, brings with it feelings of victory and bravery. It suggests you are inventive, persuasive, and idealistic. It shows to take the challenge head on and do not be scared to show a little authority.

This card, when reversed, represents sarcasm and reckless, impulsive behavior. It suggests one to be foolish and impatient. It represents someone who is arrogant and overbearing.

Symbolism:

The knight of swords asks that you use your thoughts and actions to bring about change. The grey horse and armor show an ambition, wisdom, and willingness to let go of what is holding you back and communicate to make a better future. The red of the feather and cape show the beauty of such a decision.

Queen

This card, upright, represents subtle, yet complete autonomy. It bears traits, such as honesty and intelligence, as well as openness and directness.

Reversed, it represents the negative aspects of autonomy. These may be distance and frustrations, or even brutality and malice. It could also signify deceit and intolerance.

Symbolism:
The queen of swords gives us the motivation to walk a virtuous path. Her grey throne gives her a wise support, the clouds and birds assisting in clarity of thought. The angel and butterfly on her throne reminds us that freedom can only come by letting go of what holds us back. The peaceful blue of her robe is lined with a passionate red.

King

This card is the epitome of good authority when drawn upright. It represents an active, analytical, and fair mind. It brings forth of law and justice, someone who can expertly solve disputes.

Reversed, this card signifies someone who has let power go to their head. Their ego has grown too large, causing cruelty and judgement, leading to a lack of compassion.

Symbolism:
The king of swords reminds us that our thoughts and actions, when clearly lead through a relationship with the divine, can lead to authority and respect. The birds and clouds remind us of the clear thought needed to achieve this. The butterflies on his throne reminds us that sometimes change is necessary. His passionate red sleeves and emotional blue robe is topped with a purple cloak to remind us that, while passion is necessary in any event, it is

important to lay logical thinking over top to avoid making poor decisions or no decision at all.

The Wands Suit

Wands represent a fiery passion and are the bridge between drive and desire. All cards in this section reflect that is some way.

Ace

If drawn upright, this is a good omen for starting a new project. It represents the inspiration, creativity, and passion that will plant the seeds of success for your goals. It also can represent fertility and birth.

The reversed orientation suggests helplessness and false starts. It shows cancellation, often with selfish motives.

Symbolism:
The ace of wands represents new passions or desires. The white hand, untainted and good, personally gives us these passions from a cloud of clarity. The fact that the hand is disembodied along with the presence of Yod tells us that we were given these desires directly by the divine. The castle on the green mountain gives us hope of protection during times of strife, while the brown of the wand tells us that we can use our passions to ground us. The leaves promise growth through this mindset.

Two

When this card is drawn in the upright position, it's a good omen. You may have new goals on the horizon or even accomplish your old ones. It shows willpower and authority, courage and the power within. It shows you may have a vision you wish to achieve and that you are just daring enough to achieve it.

When drawn in reverse, this card suggests someone who longs for a position of power but lacks the drive and tools necessary to achieve this goal. It can also mean you are lacking in faith in yourself or others and can come with an air of hopelessness.

Symbolism:

The 2 of wands represents the duality of grounding ourselves in our drive, protection, and looking beyond the walls of isolation in search of the orange of adventure. The inclusion of the spherical earth in our hands further state the need of grounding ourselves before heading into the mysteries of life, represented by the ocean. Surrounding the ocean are the mountains of challenge which we are destined to face.

The idea of balanced dichotomies are further expressed through the crest of masculine roses and femininity of lilies as well as the idea of following your passions versus the danger of doing so, as represented by the red hat.

Three
When drawn upright, this card suggests you will find partnership, be that in travel or commerce. You may find a trade partner or someone who can help you in day to day life. Another possible meaning is that of confidence and faith in your decision. Your effort has led to prosperity and you will finally get to enjoy it.

The reversal of the Three of Wands suggests you have wasted your talents, seeking unrealistic goals only to become frustrated and impatient. It may also warn of those who are scheming against you and planning a betrayal further down the line.

Symbolism:
The 3 of wands represents the unity of mind, body and soul through our desires and drive to achieve them. The man in the card is examining the oceans of mystery, dotted with chips of change, as well as the challenges before him, presented as the mountains in the background.

The main colors of this card are the red, blue, brown and green, representing potential danger, thoughtfulness, safety and grounding, and hope and growth, respectively.

Four
This card, upright, represents a cause for celebration and gratification. It may suggest a clean slate on which to build your life. It represents joy and rest. When taking all these aspects

together, it may, most literally, refer to a marriage or union of people.

Reversal suggests you may be on a lengthy delay that leads to impatience and a dissolution of your inner morality. However, this card doesn't solely bring bad news, as it makes the promise of success so long as you remain patient.

Symbolism:
The 4 of wands is about the desires of the heart. The arches provide new possibilities brought about by marriage. The flowers and leaves represent the beauty and growth of this new family. The castle walls provide protection as the family carves their path in life. This can be further specified that the protection of beauty and passion, as evidenced by the presence of red roofs. The couple wear laurels, representing the victory of their union and their future.

Five
If drawn upright, do not become discouraged as you are close to success. Resolve any doubts you have by asking what you are truly hoping to achieve. You may be drawn to the discussion of some creative outlet.

If reversed, it warns that in any battle, there is bound to be stress and obstacles. However, do not let excessive competition cause turbulence or unneeded conflicts. This card may also represent indecision or trickery and deceit.

Symbolism:
The 5 of wands represents the desire of growth by having the drive to overcome the challenges represented by the mountains in the background. The colors of this card are a brown of humility, a red of passion, and a blue of unity.

Six
As you draw this card in the upright position, prepare yourself for good news or promotion in a subject. With true effort, you will attain triumph and commendation. Be courageous through the advancement towards your goal and you will be victorious.

The reversal of the Six of Wands suggests you may be meant to receive news, but this news has been delayed for some reason or another. It also warns to keep your pride and ego in check before it can lead to disappointment. Another possible interpretation of this card is fear or anxiety in yourself or others.

Symbolism:
The 6 of wands embodies the drive to achieve harmony. The inclusion of the horse further points to the ambition while the laurel suggests eventual victory. The red cloak shows a willingness to sacrifice when necessary, leading to the prosperity and growth of the green saddle blanket draped on the horse.

Seven
This card represents eventual gain when upright. You may go through many challenges, but with courage and perseverance, you will ultimately achieve victory. You will go through many obstacles, but keep your head held high and keep pushing through.

This card, reversed, suggests that you may have lost the upper hand or an opportunity due to hesitation and reluctance to make a decision. It may also suggest aggression or, conversely, a total lack of courage.

Symbolism:
The 7 of wands shows our desire to have a meaningful relationship with the divine. The man is facing challenges atop a mountain and his red pants warn of danger, but, armed with his brown, grounding passion, his green tunic gives an air of hope.

Eight
Simply put, the upright orientation of the card represents something new. This could be a new section of your life, a new relationship or partnership, or even just news, be it positive or negative. You must prepare for a journey of the mind, body, and / or spirit and be ready to act at the drop of a hat. You are destined to grow quickly.

Just as easily as good things come, the reversal of this card warns that haste can lead to poor judgement and chaos. Things may seem like they are getting out of control, or perhaps you have become stagnate due to resentment or just a lack of direction. Take some time to regain control and scope out your path.

Symbolism:
The 8 of wands represents abundance that can be achieved by pursuing our passions. We still face the hardship, represented by the mountains, but with the river's emotional stability, we will eventually prosper. The card is covered with a thoughtful blue and a hopeful green both of which are necessary to succeed.

Nine
The Nine of Wands, when drawn upright, represents the order and control brought forth by tenacity and discipline. Self-assurance can bring about the eventual victory and end of opposition needed to fully resolve a conflict.

When reversed, this card symbolizes fruitless delays and stubbornness, almost to the point of a stalemate. Adversity comes, and you need to be ready when it does. Suspicion seldom yields results unless acted upon.

Symbolism:
The 9 of wands show the recollection of the struggles we have overcome, represented by the mountains, and the prosperity that came as a result, represented by the green leaves.

Ten
Upright, this card suggests you are nearing a conclusion to your conflict, even if it is not the result you have been hoping for. With commitment and dedication, will yield the results. If you've lost commitment to your cause, you can expect opposition to reign supreme.

When reversed, make sure your talents and abilities are appreciated. If you are being worked to the bone with little to no result, is it worth the exhaustion and illness? A gross misuse of talent can lead to a struggle that you are not even aware exists.

Symbolism:
The 10 of wands tells us of the satisfaction acquired when pursuing or receiving our desires. The town that the moon is approaching

shows our eventual abundance, while the brown of the wands remind us to be humble as we sprout the leaves of growth.

Page

Upright, this card states that for positive resolutions to come forth, one must be ambitious and bold. They must be lively and seek adventure. Good communication is represented by this card, as is the disclosure of news, good or bad. Like the Four of Wands, this card represents new beginnings, a clean slate.

The reversal establishes a specific type of news to be given, bad news. Indecision leads to hesitation. Hesitation can lead to gossip and stress. Be careful what is said behind your back and what news spreads about you.

Symbolism:
The Page of Wands brings news of our desires coming to fruition. The feather furthers this idea of communication while e salamander fuels our drive. Within the desert are pyramids to represent this development. The orange represents adventure along the way to our goal, but when tied to the red and tallow, warn of the dangers of losing ourselves to the pleasures of our worldly desires.

Knight

This card, upright, suggests a physical relocation of oneself, be it by travel or a permanent change of residence. This is not meant to be met with fear, but instead with eagerness as you travel into the unknown world around you.

When reversed, this card signifies acting on reckless impulses due to envious thoughts or restlessness of mind, spirit, or body. These impulses may lead to violence or unneeded conflict. Make sure to think your choices through to avoid your downfall.

Symbolism:
The Knight of Wands represents the power of our drive to achieve our deepest desires. The energy of such power is shown through the horse and armor. The horse is brown, because despite our drive being full of power, it may be subtle or hardly noticed. Again, the salamanders and the desert represent our fiery passions alongside

the red feathers of communication, and the pyramids represent out progress. The yellow represents optimism and eventual pleasure.

Queen
Given that the wands suit represents the element of fire, it comes as no surprise that the Queen's positive connotations are that of a "fiery" passion. She represents an open, loving relationship. She brings forth joy and zeal simply because she is such a fervent and passionate lover. Her tendency for spontaneity keeps the fire burning in the relationship, while her independence can provide a nice change of pace for those involved.

However, as many people know, fire can cause a lot of pain. When drawn in reverse, the Queen's negative side takes over. She can be possessive and jealous, taking control of the relationship in an almost dictatorial sense. She can be cruel and vindictive; she is very narrow-minded and stubbornly sticks to her ways.

Symbolism:
The Queen of Wands represents the desires that motivate us and our drive for success. The car graces us with its presence and knowledge of our inner strengths and abilities, represented by the lions on the throne of power. The crown tells us of our relationship with the divine and their influence as the pyramids to the side tell us of our development.
The Queen holds yellow sunflowers of optimism as the red and orange hues balance passion and possible danger. The brown of the wand reminds us to stay humble.

King
The King, upright, represents tradition and the epitome of authority. He is devoted and trustworthy. This, along with his professional and diligent demeanor, lead to him being a fantastic father figure.

However, tradition can easily corrupt the people, warns the reverse. If one is closed-minded, one can never wish to grow in society. This card represents a judgmental attitude and opposition to a new way of thinking.
Number Associations:

Kings are paternal figure of authority and ambition. They represent maturity in most cases. They have an air of respect and are generally considered wise.

Symbolism:
The King of wands reminds us of the wisdom and maturity necessary to not be overtaken by our desires. His crown unites our physical needs and our spiritual desires and weighs them against each other, balanced, as shown by the brown wand. The salamanders and the desert represent our fiery passions while the red cloak serves to remind us of the possible dangers associated with such strong desires.

The Cups Suit

Cups represent water, either cleansing or destructive, though the exact meaning of each cup depends on what is inside.

Ace

While this card, upright, represents new relationships, it also represents fulfillment and abundance. This relationship is not necessarily one of a romantic nature, as another meaning of this card is friendship. Using your intuition, humanity, and creativity, success is yours to claim. You are not quite at the resolution, but the seed of success has been planted and with work and proper effort, you can be assured to attain victory.

When reversed, the Ace represents one sided love or love lost to time and distance. This may lead to depression and a loss of faith, hardening your heart against those in need. The best advice is to work through past conflict and allow everyone involved to let it go and continue the path of life, undisturbed.

Symbolism:
The ace of cups flows over with new opportunities. From the cloud of clarity, a hand provides us with a cup overflowing with water to clean the slate. The blue of the water brings a wave of peace. A white dove, representing purity, brings us a disk showing us how everything is intertwined. Lilies sit upon lily pads, providing a feminine balance to the masculine energy of the number 1.

Two
Upright, this card represents the mending of past relationships. But for harmony to occur, you must accept yourself and deeply understand your inner workings. Doing this will lead to resolution with no clear loser, as you are united in harmony and love.

Simply put, this reversal marks the end of a relationship through break up or even divorce. Many fights may have led to this outcome, stemming from confusion and blatant differences in ideals and morality.

Symbolism:
The 2 of cups presents us with the dichotomy between a passionate red and a peaceful blue. It also highlights the duality within the balance of a caduceus. The lion head atop the caduceus is winged, showing yet another dichotomy of fight or flight. The scene is backed by a green hill, showing the possible growth brought about by properly balancing these dichotomies.

Three
True, unbiased compromise in a community can only lead to happy times and abundance, states the upright card. This compromise can be used to increase fertility and creativity, eventually achieving the hopes and dreams of everyone involved. This is cause for celebration, especially if tied with the Empress, who increases all the aspects in multiples.

However, the reversal warns to beware the two-faced among you. They may seem happy in solace, but can actually be very tired, mentally, spiritually, and physically. Treating yourself is fine in moderation, but do not allow that to overtake your life and morph to greed and jealousy.

Symbolism:
The 3 of cups provides us with the rewards we reap when we unite body, mind, and spirit. The vegetables and grapes promise rewards of pleasure, as does the use of orange and yellow. The use of flowers and the color red show beauty and growth.

Four

If drawn upright, it may be time for a change of scenery. Closely examine the conflict at hand from the perspective of another, either another party involved or an unrelated third party. With proper evaluation, you will begin to see things as they are, making victory all but guaranteed. New possibilities lie on the horizon if you can only allow yourself to see them and take them up.

If drawn reversed, avoid spoiling yourself. Whether this stems from a search for material wealth to bring happiness or just a cure to boredom, overindulgence leads to a hard time in the future. Material wealth won't bring much joy for long, and the sense of boredom will creep back over time. Do not act immature and reckless as this is a straight path to failure and loss.

Symbolism:
On the 4 of cups, the divine is directly giving us clarity and stability. It suggests to get over the mountain of challenges, we should let go.

The blue background suggests thoughtfulness, while the yellow cups on green grass gives us hope for a happy future.

Five
The upright card suggests you reassess the situation. Take a step back and look to your past experiences for guidance. Perhaps you have missed a key piece to the puzzle that has led to stagnation and lack of progress made to your ultimate goal.

This card, when reversed, brings with it a sense of loss or bad luck. Perhaps you feel unfulfilled in your current partnership or have regret from a partnership long since passed. This can cause great emotional turmoil. Take a step back and work through those problems as a vital first step to tackling the conflict at hand.

Symbolism:
The 5 of cups present us with a challenge to overcome. The castle in the background would provide protection if we could overcome the river of emotion blocking our path. The bridge in the background give a possible path, but the grey hue hints at indecision.

The black cloak gives an air of finality while the blue hues provides us with the thoughtfulness needed to overcome our emotions. The green surrounding the castle give us hope of prosperity when we can get to the protection the castle provides.

Six
Upright, your past will come to visit, but it has not malicious intent. It can bring with it joy and the key to your future success. This card also represents good will and harmony in the household. It also suggests trying to find happiness in the simpler parts of your day to day life. Appreciate the simple gestures.

However, reversal warns too much nostalgia can lead to stagnation in your current life. Appreciate your past but look to your future. Nostalgia is great in small doses, but do not let it impede you on your path to success.

Symbolism:
The 6 of cups provides us with success and harmony. The innocence of both the child and the lilies he is giving out is protected within the castle walls. If we give our creative ideas, represented by the flowers, to others and view the world through a lens of beauty and passion that the children wear on their heads in the form of red hoods, it will eventually lead to the happiness suggested in the overwhelming amount of yellow on the card.

Seven
Drawn upright, dream big and work toward your goal. It is okay if it seems daunting at first; allow your imagination to run wild. You have a freedom in the choices you make in life. Make them count. It is great to have high aspirations, as those who do not are never truly fulfilled.

Drawn reversed, do not overestimate your abilities when setting goals. The delusion of grandeur, when tied with the allure of worldly goods will lead to the wrong choices that cause your demise.

Symbolism:
The 7 of cups promises wisdom and happiness through the use of yellow, but tells us those things can easily be corrupted with

emotion by inclusion of the blue background. Each cup represents another thing to help us achieve those goals. The snake and dragon promise wisdom and power. The castle promises protection. The jewels suggest wealth, the laurel promises victory. The angel promises messages to help guide us. All of these sit atop a cloud which offers clarity on the situation.

Eight
Upright, this card marks a turning point in your life. Out with the old and in with the new, that is to say you must first get rid of the things that are causing stress before accepting new, wonderful things into your life. This can be breaking ties with an old partner or changing your course in life. This is not meant to be feared as it represents a positive change.

When drawn in reverse, this card suggests you may have set unrealistic and unachievable goals or have an unhealthy attachment to material goods. This dissatisfaction may lead to negligence and thoughtless behavior along with the unease of the mind, body, and / or spirit. The card also suggests delusion so tread carefully.

Symbolism:
The 8 of cups offer abundance and power, but tells of a possible danger of indulging too deeply by way of the red cloak. The man carries a staff for stability and support as he takes his solitary trek towards the happiness of the divine, represented by the sun and moon in yellow. He is following a path of self-discovery through the cleansing and water surrounding him, the blue representing the thoughtfulness of this trek through the mind and spirit.

Nine
This card brings with its upright position good tidings. You will experience a great relief and contentment with what you have, while also having a surplus of what you need. Your hopes and dreams will come to fruition and you will reign victorious over your impasses.

When reversed, the man is cast in a new light. He selfishly holds on to his cups in a protective manner. The card suggests that you may have blamed others for a burden that was yours to bear and as such, suffered some material loss. The card also suggests pride and extravagance but warns these can quickly get out of hand when not kept in check.

Symbolism:
The 9 of cups offers us a place of rest and reflection, by way of the associated number as well as the bench. The feather in the hat shows inner communication and the surroundings of red and yellow represents a beautiful positivity during this recollection.

Ten
This card upright represents, as depicted in the imagery, a successful, happy family life; one of honor, peace, surplus, and overall satisfaction. This card also represents unending success and eternal friendship.

When reversed, this card takes a different meaning entirely. While it means breaking routine, which is hardly a negative thing, with it comes misery and a household in shambles. It also represents a loss of friendship and suggests that, perhaps, someone you view as a friend is scheming against you.

Symbolism:
The 10 of cups provides us with energy and potential. The rainbow along with the blue sky give us peace, while the arch gives us a new life path or possibility concerning our emotional stability, represented by the river. The inclusion of the green grass provide us with hope of future growth and potential.

Page
Upright, this card represents a bringer of good news. It also represents a loving, caring, and pleasant individual involved in creative or artistic endeavors.

However, when this card is reversed, it shows an immature person, lacking in responsibility. While the seduction of childish behavior or diversion from what is considered normal may pull the more insecure of us, stand strong. Do not let selfishness overtake you. A childish side is fine in small quantities, like many other things. Do not let this get in the way of your success.

Number Associations:
The Page represents youth and earth. They are often used to announce the arrival of news.

Symbolism:
The page of cups promises longevity and innocence. The lilies and pink tunic suggest the purity of a child. The blue water provides cleansing peace while the fish gives us subconscious messages through which we can succeed.

Knight

As the Knight parades into the town, his upright card represents an arrival, either with news or another person. He brings with him invitations and a chance at advancement. With proper encouragement, success will follow. His card can also represent intuition or a simultaneous and immediate attraction between two people.

When his card is drawn in reverse, he suggests a sly individual, capable of using illusions and deceit to abuse and manipulate someone's emotions. Be wary of who you trust and keep an eye on your mental well-being.

Symbolism:
The knight of cups gives us power and ambition. The grey horse gives us ambition and wisdom. The armor provides protection while the wings atop the helmet suggest flight or divinity. There are challenges we must face when we cross the river of emotions blocking the way, but the subconscious messages the fish provides may help lead the way.

Queen

Like many cards in the Cups suit, the Queen ties into the home and family. Her devotion, when tied to her compassionate and sensitive nature causes her to be the epitome of maternal figures. She cares deeply about others and, as such, is loved and adored by those around her. She's compassionate yet intuitive. This card in its upright position also suggests psychic ability.

When reversed, the Queen doesn't become her exact opposite. She does become unscrupulous and illogical, unfaithful and arrogant, but that's not entirely the opposite of what she was before. She exemplifies how good traits can easily become corrupt. Beware losing your ground in reality. Think all choices through to completion and take the effect on other into account.

Symbolism:
The queen of cups offers us ideas and motivation using her logic and problem solving, represented by the color purple. A river of emotional stability flows in front of her, blue with thoughtfulness. Her throne shows her authority over the topics she speaks of and her crown suggests a relationship with the divine in order to provide quality advice.

King
The King, when upright, is a romantic man. He's a good speaker and responsible with a deeply philosophical nature. He is creative and artistic with enough ambition to accomplish the goals he sets. He is a natural teacher and negotiator who, while educated beyond many people around him, is still compassionate. He may be religious or cares deeply about religion.

If you remove his compassion for others, you are left with a man whose intelligence has led to a lack of honor and morality. He is unjust and, as such, commonly fails at compromises. Keep your mind and mouth in check.

Symbolism:
The king of cups provides authority and fosters ambition. His authority is clearly seen as he sits atop a throne, yellow scepter in hand, promising an optimistic approach. The fish behind him brings subconscious messages, hidden within a sea of mystery. The boat suggests support in the emotional blue tide.

The Pentacles Suit

The pentacles represent earth and, by extension, grounding, stability, security, and nature. All cards in this suit will, in some way, allude to at least one of these traits.

Ace
Upright, this card suggests good opportunities with a healthy start. It suggests an investment, sowing the seeds of success. It represents grounding of a situation.

Like many cards, reversing the Ace of Pentacles suggests a problem that needs fixing. In this case, perhaps your greed has led to excess caution and worry of loss. Being materialistic will eventually lead to harmful decisions. Keep your greed and your relationship to the physical realm in check.

Symbolism:
The ace of pentacles offers the opportunity for new wealth and financial stability. The roses represent life and the green hedge arch represents the hope for new paths and guidance. The cloud from which the white hand extends shows a clear plan for success, as the hand is giving us a pentacle for wealth and security. The garden in the foreground show abundance while the lilies represent purity. Along the path in the distance, there are many ups and downs, clear sky suggests a happy outcome.

Two
The Two of Pentacles is a playful card when upright, representing change and adaptability while multitasking. Do not allow everything around you to stress you out. Be playful in your approach and do not take on too many tasks at once.

When reversed, the playful side of this card points to being used as a way to procrastinate. You may feel overwhelmed and have dealt with many delays in the past. Procrastination is not always not working. Sometimes, you have taken on too much and cannot get anything done well. Both are equally troubling, and need worked through

Symbolism:
In the 2 of pentacles, a pair of them reside in the loops of infinity. This suggests that in both the beginning and the end, you will be prosperous and safe. The ocean in the background warns of uncertainty and mystery, but the boats residing in it give a place of support.

Colors associated with this card are as follows: blue shows the overall peace in a mysterious world. Red shows possible danger, but, when grounded with the brown, lends itself more toward necessary sacrifice and beauty.

Three
Drawing this card in its upright position suggests teamwork and employment. Perhaps a new project or goal is on the horizon. Do not be afraid to ask for or to offer assistance as many heads cause the planning process to go much more quickly.

When drawn in reverse, this card suggests that, perhaps, there is turmoil within a work group you are involved with or, perhaps, you do not have the support needed to complete a task, project, or goal. Watch for people who are uncooperative and try not to make criticism too harsh, as that will lower productivity.

Symbolism:
The 3 of pentacles promises stability and security through the unification of mind, body, and spirit. The bench gives a place of rest while the hammers show the work we need to put in to succeed. The arch shows our path through the rose of life. The arch is grey, pushing toward the idea of wisdom from the path ahead.

Four
This upright card, as the man depicted shows, represents caution and the protection of precious resources. It may symbolize some sort of savings or boundaries that need to be acknowledged. It represents stability in life.

Quite the antithesis to its upright counterpart, this reversal represents a lack of borders and boundaries and reckless abandon in regard to resources. However, it may represent greed and an unnecessary and selfish hoarding of resources.

Symbolism:
The 4 of pentacles requires love and kindness to receive the stability of the pentacles themselves. The bench offers a place to reflect on the town in the background, suggesting you may have an

abundance. The grey could be your indecision or, when tied with the black, may suggest wisdom kept secret. The yellow and red tells us that, though you may need to sacrifice a little, it will lead to overall wealth and happiness.

Five
When this card is drawn in either orientation, it represents financial burden and possible unemployment. While some people believe that upright means you will have support and reversed means you will not, the overall meaning of this card remains unchanged regardless of orientation. It may also suggest that you are focusing too much on the problem without truly looking for a solution.

Symbolism:
The 5 of pentacles tells of the challenges needing to be faced in order to gain stability. The snowy landscape with black background present a scene of struggle and finality, but with the inclusion of the stained glass, it reminds you to take a step back and view the whole picture. When you take the advice, you may find that the treacherous snowfall is untainted and perfect or the yellow light shining through brings wealth or happiness when you view things optimistically.

Six
This card, in its entirety represents the balance and dichotomy of giving and getting. Upright, this card represents charity and generosity without a second thought. This could mean that you need to take what you are given and be thankful, or it may suggest that you need to give more to your community and those around you.

Reversed, this card suggests debt because of taking too much and giving too little, or it suggests a possible hoarding of wealth and greed. Someone is expecting handouts they do not deserve. Possible corruption and exploitation may be involved, suggesting bribery or blackmail.

Symbolism:

A big idea in this card is that of harmony and balance. The scales and number represent this well as the castle provides protection to those who take a step back.

The purple stripes show a careful examination of the situation to come to a logical conclusion. The red suggests personal sacrifice in favor of those in need to lead to the eventual happiness of yellow.

Seven
This orientation simply represents trial and error. Perhaps you have not been able to resolve conflict regardless of what you try. This card suggests taking a step back and assessing the situation. Perhaps you could even get the feedback of people you can trust. With patience you will find the solution, it may just take a few more failures first.

Albert Einstein once said, "The definition of insanity is doing the same thing over and over again, but expecting different results," and that is exactly what this reversal represents. You may be ready to give up, but if you take the feedback you've received or witnessed yourself, you may approach success. Make sure your priorities are in order and you deal with each aspect of the conflict thoroughly.

Symbolism:
The 7 of pentacles represents divine gifts of stability. The green leaves of the bush on which the pentacles set represent growth and prosperity.The mountains are far in the background show struggles to come in the future but the yellow and orange tell of a positive outcome for the adventure life takes you on.

Eight
Upright, this card represents repetition. If you are doing meaningful and precise work, you can expect success with proper dedication. It also may suggest you need to stock up on the resources at your disposal. You never know when things will run out.

This reversal represents the corners cut when you lack the skills to make any progress in the work you do. This may cause you to feel unfulfilled. It may also suggest that you are probably not going to get a much hoped for promotion or raise. It represents stagnation in life and unneeded stress. Take care of yourself. You may need to take time off work or maybe you are not giving enough of yourself and as such, not doing as good a job as you could.

Symbolism:
The 8 of pentacles show that the way to achieve success, abundance, and stability is through hard work. The path of life shown in the background leads to a castle representing your goals. With the hammer meaning physical labor and yellow meaning wealth and happiness, it's easy to see that you need to work toward achieving your goals rather than expecting them to be handed to you on a silver platter.

Nine
Upright, this card means you have worked hard, and you now get to reap the fruit of you labor. This is what the Nine of Pentacles represents. With proper discipline and autonomy, you will receive the success you have earned.

However, this card may also suggest that you are not self-sufficient. You rely too much on others and will not receive success in this manner.

When reversed, this card suggests you may not value your self-worth as much as deserved. You may rely too heavily on material goods to bring you happiness but find that everything falls just short. You may be craving your independence and resisting true pleasure to try to achieve that independence. Or, alternatively, you may be expecting someone else to care for you and as such, have lost some of the dignity involved in self-sufficiency.

Symbolism:
The 9 of pentacles represents planning for success in the future. The garden of grapes show a growth and abundance of luxury. The snail at the bottom states that you need to rely on yourself mostly, while the bird shows that communication is key to succeeding. The castle walls provide protection on your quest for success.

The green of the leaves show money and overall prosperity. The yellow and red dress shows that optimism can lead you to success and beauty.

Ten
The upright orientation suggests the permanence of a legend and the legacy of your ancestors far after they have passed. It also represents wealth and heirlooms, perhaps, that of which was passed down through your family. Make sure, however, you appreciate the wealth of knowledge passed down, and not only that of material goods.

Reversed, it suggests a rejection or even outright rebellion against tradition. This may be a good thing, depending on the values you are denouncing. However, it may also lead to tension between family members and eventual exile of the rebellions.

Another possibility is that someone is hoarding resources while members of their family suffer. It is a direct disregard to blood and compassion.

One final possibility is that your family lacks tradition and new ones should be formed to further tie you together as one.

Symbolism:
The 10 of pentacles represent stability and success by way of opportunity. Within the castle gates, everyone is protected and the idea of civilization is everywhere around. Domesticated dogs give this same idea of civilization and protection. The old man wears a cloak with grapes and leaves, a sign of luxury and health long since passed. The child, on the other hand, is a blank slate and can choose the stability of tradition passed down by the old man, or travel through the arch, carving himself a new path.

Colors associated with this card are they yellows of optimism and pleasure, the greens of prosperity and growth, and the reds of danger, sacrifice, and beauty.

Page
The upright Page of Pentacles is a very kind, yet practical, student. He is more than willing to do hard work for the reward of knowledge but is very cautious. He is an excellent friend and could

possibly represent a new opportunity on the horizon, be it educational, professional, or social.

When reversed, his immature side shines through, ignoring safety and productivity in lieu of childish behaviors, squandering money and lacking focus on a task. This card may suggest that you are not taking your education seriously or that you are having difficulty planning your finances. It may also mean that someone has big dreams and plans for the future but are not making any steps in that direction.

Symbolism:
The page of pentacles suggests stability and longevity due to youth. The mountains in the background represent the struggle, but adorned with a hood in red to view the world through a lens of passion and beauty, the young man keeps his eyes on the goal of stability in the world. The flowers around him show the growth and beauty of the man while the yellow covering the card shows the man's optimism. His red leggings show that he is well aware of the possible danger, but chooses to prioritise grounding himself through his brown boots and focusing on growth and his hopeful nature with his green tunic.

Knight
The upright Knight represents a loyal and dependable friend or worker. He works hard with an astute attention to detail. He may be a bit slow moving, but he is cautious and reliable. He can be considered quite boring, but he will always give a well thought out, logical answer to a question or problem. His past experiences are expertly woven into his present abilities.

The negative aspects of the Knight of Pentacles relate directly to him being overly cautious. He may be a perfectionist and is constantly second guessing himself and others. This causes all progress to trudge by at a snail's pace. This can seem like a standstill, but progress is still technically made.

The reversal can suggest that maybe you place menial things in either too high or too low regard. You may feel apathetic to things such as your health because your life just doesn't feel interesting.

Take time to examine both your present situation and the future you strive for and find a way to progress things in a logical sense.

Symbolism:
The knight of pentacles shows the idea of power by way of grounding and security. He sits atop a black horse, hiding his true energy. His armor is topped with a red tabard to represent the sacrifices he has made along the way. He is prepared to face the struggles of the mountains in the distance but looks to the pentacle, as he knows he is safe in his grounding and secure in his footing. The background is a bright yellow to remind us that, in order to attain happiness and pleasure, we must see things in an optimistic light.

Queen
As with the Queens of other suits, the upright Queen of Pentacles is a nurturing and protective mother. She can be considered the homemaker. Given that Pentacles represent the Earth, she can be considered very down to earth and fertile. She is both logical and emotional in perfect harmony. This allows her to not only care deeply for the environment, but also make plans to fix what is wrong in the world around her.

When she is drawn in reverse, she warns to examine your place in the physical world and your relationship with it. You may not be caring for yourself or the world around you and have become unhealthy. Make sure that the things you find pleasant are healthy in the long run. If they are used to cover up a problem, you need to fix the problem at the roots, rather than smothering it with temporary happiness.

Symbolism:
The queen share secrets of the wisdom of grounding yourself for stability and security. Like all other royalty, her throne shows her authority over the concepts she covers and her crown hints at a strong relationship with the divine. Though her green veil suggests secrets of growth and prosperity, we can see her face and she is ready to tell all who are willing to lend their ears to hear her. The river of emotions in the background ebbs and flows around the struggles, represented by the mountains.

By her feet, we see the reason she shares her secrets, a rabbit, representing family and stability. The garden around her further supports ideas of growth and abundance and hints to the creativity of her ideas. Her dress is red, showing how passionate she is to help those she considers family, and given her optimistic worldview, shown by the bright yellow sky, it can be assumed that her "family" does not end with blood relatives and extends to all who would have her.

King
The upright King is ambitious and stubborn. As such, he has acquired the wealth and overall success he set out to find. He is cautious in his spending of resources, but occasionally splurges for additional comfort in life. He seems generous on the outside, often being charitable, but if an exchange does not provide something for him, the exchange will not happen.

He is very thoughtful and considerate as leader of the household. He is calm and slow to anger, but anger will still fall when his loved ones act irrationally.

Drawing this card in reverse could suggest that you are putting worldly artifacts at the top of your priorities, and that is not necessarily a good thing. You may be splurging more than is healthy or putting your earnings above all else in your life. You may have lost your way in life in pursuit of income and splurging. Perhaps you should look into free activities that can bring happiness like hiking and enjoying nature.

Symbolism:
The king of pentacles shows the wisdom of stabilizing yourself before following your drives and ambitions. His crown suggests he has been gifted wisdom from the divine and the throne shows that they have given him their support in telling those around him his secrets. His robe is adorned with grape patterns, showing the luxury in which he has lived, but the red scarf shows that he is well aware of the possible danger that comes with his position. He also wears armor, showing his preparation for such danger.

The bronze bull heads atop his throne and the silver ones on the armrests show his overall power and wealth, while the castle behind him shows the protection he is more than happy to provide. On the tip of his scepter is a perfect sphere. This shows completion of his goals and the coloration- yellow- shows that his is happy about the outcome as it may have brought with it wealth and pleasures, both of the world and of the emotions.

He sits in a garden to show his creativity with many leaves surrounding him to allude towards his health and the growth of his kingdom. This idea is further supported by the sheer amount of green on the card, representing prosperity and growth, as well as the hope for a continued happiness in the future.

The purple in the card shows that the king of pentacles is a logical man. He is a master at problem solving and, when tied with the divine blessing to share his secrets, more than willing to help those around him.

CHAPTER 7
The Lay Of The Land

Single Card

While the most basic "spread" is to ask a question, either open ended or direct, and draw a single card for your answer, most people do not consider this to be an actual spread, given it only uses one card. It is still extremely helpful if you do not feel you need or have time for a full spread.

Three Card

This spread is best used to overcome a specific problem or to just get an overview of your life on your current path. As the name suggests, there are only three cards. These cards are set in a line, usually horizontal, but vertical works as well.

The first card represents the past. If you were asking about a specific problem, this could be what started the problem in the first place, giving some insight on how to fix it. If you were asking about your life, this will most likely just be a quick overview of your life up to this point.

The second card (aka the middle card) represents the present. It can show what's on your mind and how you feel about a current topic, even if that feeling is subconscious. If asking about a problem, it can also show the current state of the problem or even how any other person(s) involved may feel about the problem.

The final card represents the future. If you continue on the path you are currently on, what lies ahead? If asking about your life, this could be a good time to stop a bad habit, if you do not like the card of the future. If asking about a problem, this could tell you what lies ahead on your current path or give insight as to how to solve the problem.

The Celtic Cross

Perhaps the most commonly used spread is that of the Celtic Cross. This spread uses ten cards.

The first card goes in the center and represents your current situation. It tells what the problem is and what factors surround it.

The second card crosses the first horizontally. It is always considered upright. It tells you the core obstacle and what is preventing you from achieving your goal or finding the answer to your question. If it seems to be something positive, it could actually be jealousy of the situation in question.

The third card goes above the first and represents how your subconscious is influencing your question. It can be used to show what you desire at your deepest levels. If the second card is positive and this card is negative, it may be saying that you are creating your own negative outcome with negative thoughts, thinking you can never achieve the positive connotation of the second card.

The fourth card goes below the first. This card shows the tools you have to work with to overcome the obstacle. This can be negative aspects, but negative aspects can eventually accomplish a positive goal with work. Alternatively, if the second was positive and both the third and fourth are negative, the aspects of this card may be what is stopping you from achieving your goal or finding answers.

The fifth card usually goes to the right of the first. Many people, however, place it to the left as it shows the past. These could be issues that haven't been dealt with correctly or the inspiration needed to achieve your goal.

The sixth card usually goes to the left of the first, but is sometimes placed to the right, as it is your guiding light and represents the possible future. Either way, the sixth card should finish the basic cross with the first and second card forming the middle. This card tells what lies at the end of your current path. It is used as a warning or to give a sense of comfort in your choices.

The next three cards form a vertical line to the right of the cross and address possibilities to better your situations and accomplish your goal or receive the answers you crave.

The top of these is the seventh card. This card represents your attitude toward the situation. If you have a negative attitude about things, it may be best to try to clear your mind and deal with your outlook on the situation before dealing with the situation itself.

Below that is the eighth card. It represents the energies of your surroundings and of those you surround yourself with. If the cards suggest that this is the underlying problem, it may be best for you to distance yourself from these influences.

Next in the column is the ninth card, representing your hopes and fears. Many times, your unrealistic dreams or fears can be the biggest obstacle in accomplishing your goals. It is always good to analyze these and insure they are not impeding progress.

Finally, at the bottom of the column is the tenth card. This represents the final outcome. Based on your current trajectory, how can you expect this problem to end? If you do not like the outcome listed, perhaps you need to analyze the rest of the spread and change the things that may lead to that outcome.

The Tree of Life

This spread is commonly used to make a decision between two possibilities. After all the cards are laid out, you will have 3 cards forming a trunk and 7 cards forming the branches, 3 per side with 1 in the top center, forming an arc. You do not place these cards in the most obvious way, so pay attention.

The first and second cards go side by side with space for a third in the center. You can approximate. It doesn't have to be perfect. These two cards represent your two options.

Next, cards three and four go under one and two with slightly more space in between. These represent the pros and cons of a choice. Each card can represent both the pros and cons of the card above it, or you can analyze one specific choice and have the pros on the left and the cons on the right. The first way is more often used, but either have potential.

Cards five and six go below three and four. These represent your thoughts and feelings, even subconscious ones. These can be read the same as before, either each card representing the choice above or one card representing thoughts and the other representing feelings.

The seventh card forms the base of the trunk or the roots. This card represents the things that tie you down, be it physical ability or the influences around you. All in all, it represents your worldview.

The eighth card goes above the seventh and represents how you view the situation as a whole. It represents your personal opinion. This is not to be confused with the fifth and sixth cards, as those represent your thoughts and feelings for a particular option.

The ninth card goes above the eighth. This card represents your heart. What feels right? Try to connect to your innermost self in search for your answer. This card represents how to best, or worst, do that. Perhaps it states that you need to disconnect from yourself, or maybe, you never connected to yourself in the first place.

The tenth card goes atop the arc of leaves and represents your spiritual influence. It can tell you of the potential growth or help you better understand your spiritual goals.

The Pyramid Spread

This spread is used to check in on your life and accomplishments from time to time. It is not a spread you do for the same person often but gives milestones that you may have passed and lessons you may have learned. It consists of ten cards.

The first row has only one card. This card represents where you currently stand in life. If it is a negative card, perhaps you have an unresolved problem that needs brought to light.

The second row consists of two cards. Each card represents a life lesson you have learned, be it from experience or another person.

The third row has three cards, each representing influences or beliefs you have based on the lessons learned thus far.

The final row consists of four cards representing how things are currently going and offer insight to future lessons and problems that may arise.

The True Love Spread

This spread allows you to evaluate a current relationship and help determine if you have found "true love". When completed, this spread will form a heart with only six cards. It is important that you do not take this spread as absolute law, but instead talk about possible issues brought up and work them out.

The first card represents you and how you currently feel in the relationship. It tells how you deal with things and how you feel it will end, if you feel it will at all.

The second card goes beside the first and represents all the things as the first, but in your partner's perspective.

The third card starts a second row and is slightly to the left of the first card, but still under it. It represents connection and common ground. What do you have in common?

The fourth card goes beside the third, positioning itself under, yet between cards one and two. This is the core of the heart. It represents the strengths in the relationship.

The fifth card goes to the right of the fourth. It represents the weakness of the relationship.

The final card goes directly beneath the fourth, making the point of the heart. This card represents the things that need to be addressed and gives insight to whether or not your relationship will last on its current path.

The Success Spread

This spread suggests the best way to overcome an obstacle when you have no clue where to start. It identifies your skills and the tools available and tells you how you may be able to use them to overcome your problem. This spread consists of 5 cards.

The first card represents your obstacle and major concerns about that obstacle. It tells you what you are facing in more detail than you perhaps already know.

The second card is placed to the left of the first and adds detail to the first card. How is your problem manifesting? How prominent is it in making you follow a specific path?

The third card goes to the right of the first. This tells the hidden facts that are not easily found about your problem. This card is imperative to overcoming your situation, as you cannot truly fight without knowing what you are up against.

The fourth card goes above the second. This card represents new aspects that can aid in your growth and eventually lead to your success.

The final card goes below the second. It can either represent what you need to do or what you may need to stay away from in order to attain success in your endeavors.

The Career Path

This spread is useful if you wish for a change of scenery regarding your current job, be it finding a new one, or changing positions within your current job. It consists of seven cards, forming three rows. Unlike many other spreads, the cards of each row are placed right to left.

The first card is furthest to the right of the top row. It helps give insight as to if you are truly happy with your current job. It's generally straightforward, but in some cases may require more personal introspection.

The second card is placed to the left of the first and tells how you can further your career. A positive meaning may be saying that you are meant to be where you are and should stay in that position. A negative card will usually signify what kind of change you need to make.

The third card is the only card in the middle row. It represents unwavering stagnation in your work life. Even if the first row seems to point to changing jobs, this card may give insight into what sort of similarities you should search for.

The fourth card is the rightmost card of the bottom row. It represents your current performance. It also gives insight into why your performance may be this way.

To the left of the fourth card, the fifth represents the aspects that need to change or improve. This card can be major, suggesting a change in careers, or minor, suggesting subtle changes that will make you happier and healthier in your current position.

Continuing to the left, the sixth card tells of past experiences that may be affecting your current professional experiences and status. This card is an extremely important card and should be reviewed and interpreted carefully.

Finally, the seventh card lies farthest to the left on the bottom row. As with most spreads, this last card represents the outcome based on your current path or what the outcome will most likely be if you follow the guidance given.

Finding Love

This spread can be one of the harder ones to master interpreting, as you do not want to make things so specific, you accidently block out the person fate intended, but you do not want to be so broad, anyone will fit the description. This spread requires 5 cards.

Card number one represents how ready you will be for a relationship or how ready you currently are. Are you wanting an actual relationship, or does your desire for a fling masquerade as wanting an actual relationship? Will you accept the relationship with open arms, or will you take a while to warm up to the idea?

The second card goes to the right of the first and represents their characteristics. What features stand out the most? What will you notice first? What will they be like?

The third card goes to the left of the first. This card tells the circumstances you will meet this person under. What will you or they be going through? What is literally going on when you meet? Do you already know this person or not?

The fourth card goes above the first. This explains the characteristics of your relationship. Will it be healthy? What strengths or weaknesses will be involved?

The final card goes under the first and represents the relationship's potential. Will this relationship last? What will it be like? What are possible problems you can prepare for?

CHAPTER 8
What Am I Doing?

Before the Reading
You need to take time before the initial reading to pose your question. You may choose to hold your cards during this step or place them in front of you. Ask your question in the purest terms possible, easily showing exactly what you are asking. Invoke the Divine or Fate to show you the answers through your cards.

You also need to know which spread you plan on doing. You can choose a spread yourself or use this time to ask the Divine to lead you to the spread that will be most helpful to find your answer.

Setting Up the Spread
First, shuffle the cards. You may even cut the deck or allow the person the reading is for to do so. *Note: Allowing others to touch your cards is completely optional. Some readers feel that it is necessary to get personalized answers, while others feel the energies of other hands will confuse the cards or taint them, making them less effective until you cleanse them.*

Make sure you've followed the spread you intend to use as closely as possible. All cards at this point will be face down. Take a moment to reiterate your question and ask the Divine to use the cards before you to help guide you.

Revealing Cards and Reading the Spread
One at a time, you will focus on the meaning of a card's position as you flip the card over. Whether you flip it horizontally or vertically is up to you. You may even allow the person whom the answers are for to flip the cards themselves. You can either try to interpret the cards as they are flipped or after the entire spread is revealed.

Interpreting the Cards
Compare the meanings from Chapter 6, or your personal meanings, to what the placement represents. If you are doing the spread for someone across from you, you may choose to use the orientation of the cards from their point of view, effectively flipping each card.

Using this comparison in conjunction with the original question, try to piece together what the Divine is telling you. Many times, this story will not be obvious. You may need to use multiple meanings for multiple possibilities.

Repeat
The best way to practice your divination is to attempt often and keep track of your attempts in some form of journal. Do this often and you will develop a knack in no time.

CHAPTER 9
Practice Makes Perfect

Daily Practice
In order to get good at a skill, especially in the case of divination and Tarot reading, the most obvious first step is to practice daily or as close to daily as you can. You will most likely just start with personal readings, as it is easier to see how cards relate to you than to others.

After you get more comfortable with the cards, the next step would be to try readings for other people. It is best to try this with people you know well at first before branching out to people you may not know as well, and eventually offer readings for near complete strangers. At each of the stages of this step, make sure you are extremely comfortable with the readings before advancing to the next stage. Take baby steps. If you dive into the deep end before learning to swim, it is most likely not going to end well.

New Meanings
In any given reading, or even between readings, you may feel inclined to give a new meaning to a card based on what the Divine places in your heart and mind. This is completely okay and even encouraged. As stated in Chapter 6, many people end up giving personal meanings to their entire deck. There is, yet again, no wrong way to do things.

This is not to say you completely ignore the card drawn and come up with your own meaning on the spot every time. The card was drawn for a reason. The reason may not be the pre-set meaning, but it will have something to do with the card.

Habit Forming
Try to make the steps laid out in Chapter 8 into a habit. Part of this is practicing daily, but a lot of it is making a divination ritual. Maybe you have a specific area in which card reading is made easier.

In addition, the more you read the cards, the less you will have to look to the guidance of Chapter 6's meanings. For example, after so many times of drawing Death in its upright position, you will just know it means a sudden change without having to look up the details. This allows for quick, fluid, and often more accurate readings.

CHAPTER 10
Incorporating The Cards In Your Life

Do: Use the Cards Often
This is how you develop a knack for reading them in the first place. Without frequent usage, even on mundane things, proficiency, much less mastery, will take a long time to achieve.

Do not: Rely Too Heavily on The Cards
As mentioned in Chapter 2, the cards are meant for guidance. They are not meant to be used as an absolute. By taking the cards literally or expecting things to happen exactly as they laid out, you put yourself on a path of failure and disappointment. Some things laid out in the cards may not ever come to fruition. This is because, even subconsciously, you know the outcome of your current path and work to make it the most desirable outcome possible.

Do: Try Different Spreads
When doing readings, you want to choose the spread you feel will most thoroughly answer the question. There's not really a one-size-fits-all spread that will cover every situation. As such, you should practice multiple spreads to fill your repertoire. Even if you think you know enough different spreads, you may find a new favorite that is more useful than any of your previous spreads.

Do not: Get Discouraged
If your readings aren't 100% accurate, do not worry. Few actually are. Keep practicing your readings and interpretations. They will get better with time and effort. Many beginners will quit their attempts after a few failures. By failing, you only learn how to achieve in the future. Practice makes perfect in most aspects of life, and divination is no exception.

Do: Keep a Journal or Notebook
This journal can be used for anything related to Tarot. You can write down readings and interpretations along with the date and question and keep track of how your accuracy improves. You may write down personal meanings to cards. This is especially helpful if you've re-defined most, if not all, of your deck. You can also keep

track of your favorite spreads, noting the patterns and meanings of each card.

If you own one, this journal could actually just be your Book of Shadows or Grimoire.

Do not: Use the Cards Solely as a Fallback for Rough Times
Hopefully, you won't have many major problems in life to use the cards on. That being said, if you only use the cards during these times of turmoil, you won't be getting much practice, and you can't depend too heavily on your readings and interpretations to be as accurate as they could be. Even mundane readings, such as a one card answer to "Should I get a burger or a salad?" provides practice to your interpretations.

CONCLUSION

Thank you once again for purchasing and reading my book.

I hope I was able to explain things in a way that is easy to understand and that, by reading, you feel confident in starting your journey into divination by Tarot reading. All that remains is for you to experiment with the tips and tricks provided here and find out what works best for you.

Like most things involving the occult, things can be added or removed as you see fit. If you do not feel like a piece of information given here aligns with your path in life, feel free to disregard or change it for yourself in your journey.

Lastly, if you found this book helpful, a positive Amazon rating would be greatly appreciated. Thank you so much and I wish you happy travels ahead. Blessed be.

Book Description

Did you know that Tarot used to be a game played by royals that was lost to time? It was later unburied and eventually shifted to being one of the most popular forms of divination, untouched for decades. Shelly O'Bryan's *Tarot Reading for Dummies* includes not only a crash course history of Tarot reading, but also everything a beginner could possibly need to learn to read Tarot cards. Even if you are a different skill level, from novice to absolute expert, you can still find additional information and a handy layout for interpretations in this book.

This book gives the meanings of all 78 cards, both upright and reversed as well as going in depth into some of the symbolism behind the illustrations of each card in the Rider-Waite deck, the original and most popular Tarot deck to date.

In addition to a detailed look at every card and a history of Tarot and divination, Shelly O'Bryan has included example Tarot spreads with detailed instruction.

www.ingramcontent.com/pod-product-compliance
Lightning Source LLC
Chambersburg PA
CBHW071503070526
44578CB00001B/426